# It Happened in Moscow

"Anton Chekhov once wrote that every human being actually lives two lives: the open, public one that everyone can see, and another, hidden, the life that goes on in secret. In *It Happened in Moscow*, Maureen Klassen leads us, step by careful step, into that second, secret story of the Klassen/Reimer families. The family of Mary and C.F. Klassen escapes from Moscow to Canada and the family of Jakob J. Reimer remains in Moscow. How are these families connected? What happened to them? Where are they now? *It Happened in Moscow* answers these questions, and many more. With great grace and clarity, this book narrates how goodness and faith and love can flourish not only in Canada, but also live on and defy one of the darkest political regimes of the 20th century. Read it and be blessed."
—**Rudy Wiebe**, author, *Of this Earth: A Mennonite Boyhood in the Boreal Forest*

"What splendid love of life and what energetic writing! They held me captive in this mystery linking an eminent Canadian family to women in war-time Moscow. Mary leaps off the page, perky and full of humor. But more than that, this is intelligent well-documented writing by and about cultured and unsinkable women—Erika moves embassies and the KGB to get at the truth, and Mary and Maureen dare to become 'Gentile brides' among ethnic Mennonites."
—**Dorothy Siebert**, author, *Whatever it Takes*

"*It Happened in Moscow* is the riveting story of a family, a secret that spans Revolution and World War, and a stunning discovery. Maureen leads us beneath and beyond the story recounted in her earlier book, *Ambassador to His People*, which she wrote with her husband, Herb. In this narrative, Maureen's writing gives life to a Russian woman seeking her brother in Canada, to an intrepid man arrested by the KGB and never heard from again, and to the amazing woman at the heart of this story, her mother-in-law, Mary Brieger Klassen. This memoir attests to our human impulse to recover the truth and it demonstrates the grace to sit with the silence of the past."
—**Connie Braun**, author, *The Steppes are the Colour of Sepia*

"The story of Erika and 'Jacob's kin' will undoubtedly bring real joy and deep sadness to the hearts of readers. Very well researched and creatively written, Maureen's memoir represents a unique portrait of two families, Baltic Lutheran and Russian Mennonite, in what was clearly a most difficult experience. Questions remain, as the author points out, but the essence of the total experience of these families can be appreciated with amazement. The descended families and the larger community need to know what we are given here."
—**Lawrence Klippenstein**, director (1975–1997), Mennonite Heritage Centre, Winnipeg

"Maureen's vivid descriptions of her encounters with Russians in Moscow, following the collapse of the Iron Curtain, uncover a host of people seeking to understand the hard years under Stalinism. Maureen and her husband, Herb, make the especially intriguing discovery of Erika—a sister of Herb's brother, Harold, a sister nobody knew about. In the many revelations through this contact, Maureen also seeks to uncover the story of Herb's parents, C.F. Klassen and his wife, Mary Brieger Klassen, who met in Moscow during the mid-1920s."
—**Anne Konrad**, author, *Red Quarter Moon*

"This multi-layered memoir winds its way through the delights and tragedies of three remarkable women—Mary, Erika, and Maureen—along with their husbands, families, and friends. The author, Maureen, weaves together love and suffering, faith and despair, discovery and questions. She not only tells previously unknown stories about significant individuals, but also builds bridges of compassion and understanding towards lesser known people—those who could not escape the Soviet Union, those of Russian Orthodox faith, and others maligned during Stalin's reign of terror. Golden threads of faith, hope, and love glisten throughout this touching and poignant book."
—**Andrew Dyck**, professor, Canadian Mennonite University

# It Happened in Moscow

a memoir of discovery by

# Maureen S. Klassen

Winnipeg, MB  Goessel, KS

**It happened in Moscow: a memoir of discovery**

Copyright © 2013 the Mennonite Brethren Historical Commission of the U.S. and Canadian Conferences of Mennonite Brethren Churches (www.mbhistory.org).

All rights reserved. With the exception of brief excerpts for reviews, no part of this publication may be reproduced, stored in a retrieval system or transmitted, in whole or in part, in any form by any means, electronic, mechanical, photocopying, recording, or otherwise without written permission of the Mennonite Brethren Historical Commission of the U.S. and Canadian Conferences of Mennonite Brethren Churches (www.mbhistory.org).

Published simultaneously by Kindred Productions, Winnipeg, Manitoba R3M 3Z6 and Kindred Productions, Goessel, Kansas 67053.

Cover design by Audrey Plew.

Printed in Canada by CP Printing Solutions, Winnipeg, Manitoba R3M 3Y1.

**Library and Archives Canada Cataloguing-in-Publication Data**

Klassen, Maureen
   It happened in Moscow: a memoir of discovery / by Maureen S. Klassen.

ISBN 978-1-894791-35-9

   1. Klassen, Mary Brieger. 2. Gurieva, Erika Reimer. 3. Klassen, Maureen. 4. Mennonites--Canada--Biography. 5. Mennonites--Russia--Biography. 6. Moscow (Russia)--Biography. I. Title.

BX8143.K5473K53 2013     289.7092'271     C2013-901690-2

International Standard Book Number: 978-1-894791-35-9

Visit our website: www.kindredproductions.com

*for Herb,
companion on the journey*

*and for Jakob's grandchildren in Canada,
Irene, Rita, Randy, and Lorri*

This is a memoir of discovery. It describes my encounters with two women, Mary and Erika. As I share my memories of the role each of them played in my life, I invite you to join in the journey of discovery, exploring with me the meaning of what happened in Moscow.

*The secret things belong to the Lord our God;
but those that are revealed belong to us,
and to our children.*
—Deuteronomy 29:29

*To the living we owe compassion,
but to the dead we owe the truth.*
—Voltaire

*Maureen and Herb Klassen, 2009*

# Contents

| | | |
|---|---|---|
| Introduction | | 1 |
| 1. | Moscow Calling | 7 |
| 2. | Mary Martha Brieger | 15 |
| 3. | Discoveries | 29 |
| 4. | Harold and Erika's Correspondence | 48 |
| 5. | Mary and Jakob | 65 |
| 6. | Mary and C.F. Klassen in Moscow | 86 |
| 7. | Those That Remained | 105 |
| 8. | To the Depths | 128 |
| 9. | Return to Moscow in 1994 | 140 |
| 10. | A KGB Revelation in Moscow | 150 |
| 11. | To Ukraine in 2001 | 160 |
| 12. | The End of the Road | 171 |
| 13. | Life After Moscow | 178 |
| Epilogue: Messiah in the Kremlin | | 205 |
| Acknowledgments | | |

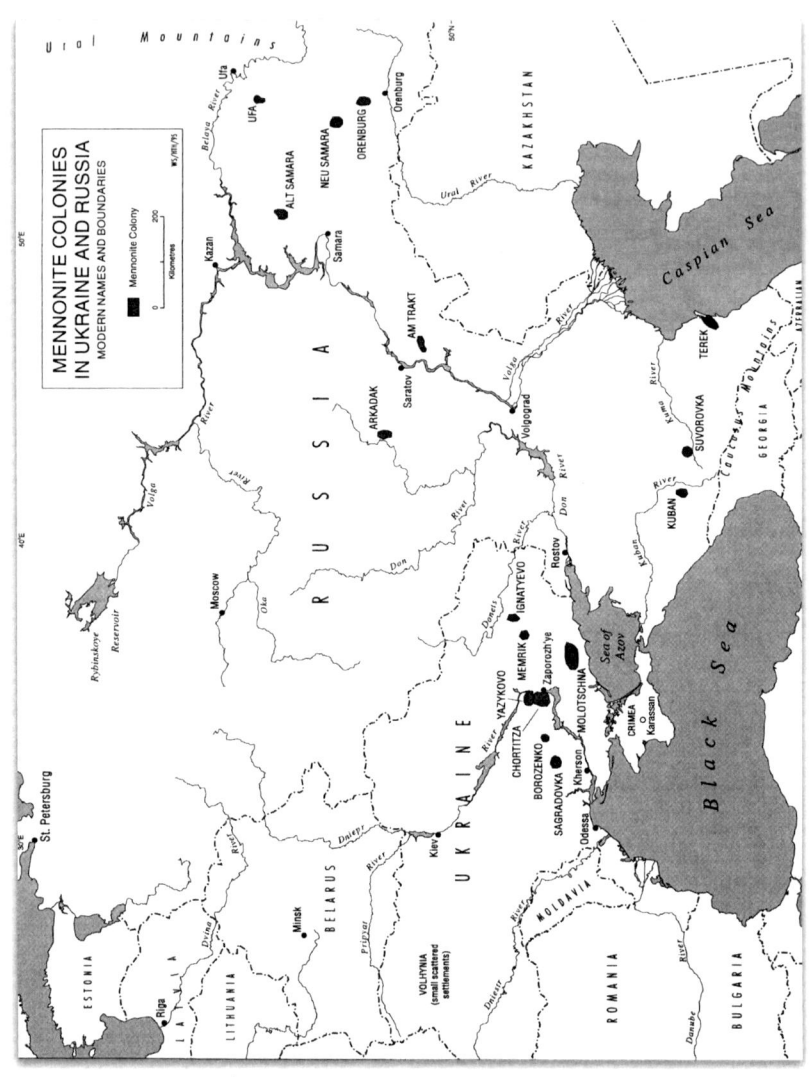

*Map of Mennonite settlements in Ukraine and Russia by William Schroeder and Helmut Huebert,* Mennonite Historical Atlas, *second edition (Winnipeg: Springfield, 1996), 14. Used with permission.*

# Introduction

The story contained in this book remained hidden for years. But we didn't go looking for it. It found us! It came to us through an unexpected telephone call in 1993, when my husband, Herb, and I were in Moscow working as volunteers for Mennonite Central Committee (MCC), an international relief agency. It was a call that would open a new and fascinating, and previously unknown, chapter in the life of my mother-in-law, Mary Brieger Klassen.

When I first met my mother-in-law, she had been a widow for six years. She impressed me as a woman of distinct style and personality as she went about her solitary life among the Mennonites of the Fraser Valley, British Columbia, where she lived. To many in Canada, she was simply known as Mrs. C.F. Klassen, wife of the man to whom they felt they owed their very existence in Canada. This Cornelius Franz Klassen, or CF as he was called, was known for his role in the great exodus of Mennonites from Russia during the 1920s, and later, in the rescue of refugees fleeing Russia through Germany in the wake of World War II.

For some, Mary was the woman who had stood tall *beside* her husband in his role as respected leader of his people. To others, she was the woman who was always there *behind* this great figure in the Mennonite story. For her children, she was all too often the woman who was left behind *without* him, to take care of the family as he responded to the demanding challenges of his responsibilities with various Mennonite organizations.

Mary and I also shared a special bond beyond the fact that her son was my new husband. We were both outsiders who had joined ourselves by choice and by marriage to this pilgrim people called Mennonites, she in the 1920s, and I in the 1960s. So she understood me and was uniquely equipped to help me transition from the English world of my youth to the Mennonite fold in Canada. She warmly welcomed me into the Klassen family. She even helped me understand the German she spoke with my husband.

Yet in all the years I knew her, she never mentioned the story contained in this book, concerning her earlier life in Moscow.

*Mary Brieger Klassen, 1920s*

In the 1980s, Herb and I wrote a book on CF called *Ambassador to His People: C.F. Klassen and the Russian Mennonite Refugees*. There we mentioned the simple fact, known within the family, that Mary had been married before she met CF. We cast a rather negative light over that aspect of Mary's life, about which we admittedly knew very little at that time. We portrayed her first husband, whose name was then unknown to us, as a man of weak character who had abandoned his young wife and child in Moscow. This, of course, helped characterize CF as Mary's rescuer. It was the way the whole episode had been viewed by many in the wider family and the Mennonite community; and we had no knowledge with which to counter it.

Then, in 1993, fifteen years later, with the revelation we received in Moscow came the possibility of understanding more about the unnamed husband, whom we now knew was a Jakob J. Reimer, and

# Introduction

why the life he shared with our mother, Mary, had been cut short. It was an opportunity to learn more about the events that had happened in Moscow during the turbulent years of the Russian Revolution; and it was time to set the record straight.

The impetus to write this book was fourfold. First, it would offer a fuller version of Mary's early life in Moscow and a chance to explore what kind of man Jakob Reimer really was.

Second, it would present an opportunity to speak at greater length about Mary herself, the inspiring woman who had stood beside CF during those tumultuous years, uncomplaining, steadfast, and resilient. Mary, whom I first met in 1959 and with whom I lived during the closing years of her life in Canada, was a woman who touched us deeply with her vitality, wit, and style, and above all her steadfast faith and courage.

Third, this memoir would give me a chance to reflect on some of our own experiences in that city of Moscow where Mary had lived. It was the place we encountered many who, like Jakob Reimer, made up that fateful group of Mennonites who were not able to escape the Soviet Union. I have called them, "Jakob's kin," or "the ones who remained."

Fourth, as a memoir of discovery on so many levels, this story would be my way of acknowledging the discoveries of another woman, Erika Reimer Gurieva, the daughter of Mary's first husband by his second wife. We came to know her through that unexpected telephone call in Moscow, and our lives became deeply intertwined for the remainder of our five-year term in that city. It was Erika whose remarkable tenacity and perseverance uncovered much of the material contained in this book, including details about her father's trial and death that brought closure to a tragic chapter in his life.

The story contained in this book breaks a long silence in the C.F. Klassen family. Over the years that followed that telephone call in Moscow, we have searched and waited for many more details to unfold, in order to fill in missing pieces of important family history and to answer many of the questions that arose for all of us. These discoveries contain unexpected but valuable information for some of our relatives concerning their true grandfather and his fate at the hands of Stalin's regime.

With the crumbling of the Soviet Union in the 1990s came the possibility of picking up such lost threads in the larger Mennonite story, including information about those who had remained in Russia. People could again ask questions about severed ties of family and friendship.

What became of the faith of those who remained? Was it lost or abandoned through the years of persecution and suffering? Did some of these people again reach out for the faith of their forebears?[1]

*Erika Reimer Gurieva, 1950s*

Any Mennonite story must be seen against the perennial Mennonite dilemma: leaving or remaining. We are grateful that our parents CF and Mary were able to leave. Many they had loved, including Jakob Reimer, remained to face an uncertain fate. We dare not read our history only through the lens of the success stories of those who emigrated and made something of their lives. Who we are as a people must embrace the lives of those who remained and suffered. So in examining the fate of some who did not make it to Canada, we gain a deeper understanding of the temptations and challenges they

---

[1] See John B. Toews, *Journeys: Mennonite Stories of Faith and Survival in Stalin's Russia* (Winnipeg: Kindred Productions, 1998); and Harry Loewen, ed., *Road to Freedom: Mennonites Escape the Land of Suffering* (Kitchener: Pandora Press, 2000).

Introduction

faced. Our corporate faith weaves together threads of gain and loss. The collective wisdom of succeeding generations encompasses both destinies. Let us not judge too harshly because of their silence. If we look back with understanding, we can move forward with courage.

*Maureen Shelagh Harvey Klassen, 1980s*

This narrative collects many fragmentary threads that may at times seem disjointed. The reason for this is that the fragments described in this book span a period of nearly one hundred years. And then these threads are interwoven with our own family's experience of discovery, during the more recent past when we lived in Russia and Ukraine. I hope that weaving all these threads together will bring a deepened understanding of the significance of what happened in Moscow nearly a century ago.

*And we will take heart for the future,*
*remembering the past.*
—T.S. Eliot

# 1

# Moscow Calling

In 1993, on a chilly April afternoon in Russia, the telephone rang in our Moscow apartment. My husband and I were living in Russia, on assignment with the Mennonite Central Committee (MCC).

"Is this Herbert Klassen?" a female voice asked in Russian.

My husband answered, also in Russian, "Yes, it is."

"Do you have a brother, Harold?"

"Yes, I do."

A further question came, "*Zhivotye escho?*" (Is he still alive?)

"Yes, he is living in Abbotsford, British Columbia, Canada."

"I am his sister, Erika."

There was a pause as Herb tried to digest this strange information. How could his brother have a sister in Russia of whom he had never heard?

Then he picked up the conversation again, beginning the long process of unraveling—a journey of discovery that was to occupy many hours over many years to come. That telephone call opened the door to a relative he'd never heard of or met and to a whole unknown chapter in the life of his mother, Mary Brieger Klassen.

How did we come to be living in Moscow at this time? And how had I, an English Methodist, born in England far away from the world of Mennonites, come to be part of a Canadian Mennonite family, the Klassens? It was a long and winding road that first led me to North America in the year 1958 and would eventually see me in Moscow during the momentous events of the Soviet Union's collapse.

The year of my birth in England was 1937. Ironically, that was the year that Russia saw the worst atrocities of the entire Soviet period. In typical English style, so different from the clannishness of Mennonites, my parents were drawn from very different places and backgrounds. My English father, James Harvey, born in central London and my mother, Margaret Veitch, born in a village in Ireland, met in a fashionable Scottish Presbyterian church in central London called Regent Square Presbyterian Church, where they were married. They also had me baptized as a baby there. We later attended a Methodist church in the small suburb of London, Potters Bar, where I grew up and came to faith.

I first heard of Mennonites while at the University of London. I had a young friend in the Methodist student fellowship who was a pacifist and had served with Quakers in a Friends Ambulance Unit in Greece alongside some American Mennonite Pax boys doing alternative service after World War II. I was already a convinced pacifist when I learned that Mennonites were conducting voluntary service work camps in post-war Europe for students and other young people. I met some of their leaders at a place called the London Mennonite Centre in Highgate, North London.

My own interest in Mennonites continued during my studies at the University of London, when I participated in several such work camps in Germany, France, and southern Austria. I also continued to become better acquainted with Mennonites and other well-known pacifists at a weekly meeting at the London Mennonite Centre. These included people like Muriel Lester, the founder of a work in the East End of London called Kingsley Hall, which was named after Muriel's brother who had died. This was the place where she had hosted the iconic pacifist, Mahatma Gandhi, during the negotiations for Indian Independence. In fact, I slept in the room he had used, when I led a work camp at Kingsley Hall with the growing group of university students who shared my interest in Mennonites. Some were from my own university and others from Cambridge University. I was the only one of that group, however, who would eventually become a Mennonite.

Since my high school days I had been fascinated by the Left Wing of the Reformation called the Anabaptists, who laid their lives down in peaceful non-resistance for their convictions about the way of Jesus. A growing conviction of my own concerning the Anabaptist peace witness stirred within me a desire to identify with this church descended from those sixteenth-century martyrs.

In the ongoing adventure of my life, I crossed the ocean after graduating from the University of London to study at Goshen College, Indiana. Wanting to learn more about Mennonite history and theology, I was persuaded by Harold Bender, the seminary dean, to enroll in the seminary. I was the only full-time female student! He suggested I should take as many courses as possible from a bright, young professor who had just returned from Europe, John Howard Yoder. He became a lifelong friend and mentor. When Herb and I were married at Reba Place Fellowship in August 1959, it was Harold Bender who officiated and John Howard Yoder who gave one of the sermons.

Growing up I had a fascination for all things Russian, their literature and their music. I was especially interested to learn about the group of Russian Mennonites who descended from Dutch and Germanic Anabaptists. In the eighteenth century, at the invitation of the Russian Tsarina, Catherine the Great, these Mennonites emigrated from Prussia (now Poland) to Russia, in order to settle and farm the fertile plains of Ukraine. In my studies, I wrote a paper on the settlements they established there and I was impressed with their peaceful lifestyle and accomplishments in education and agriculture. The descendants of these Mennonite settlers who immigrated to Canada after the Russian Revolution and the Russian Civil War in the 1920s are the people group into which my husband was born.

Increasingly drawn into the world of the Mennonites, I understood that I was choosing a lifelong association with a stream of history that would provide endless fascination and a reservoir of stories of courage and faith. These would preoccupy me for decades to come.

Studying, however, was not my only interest. I wanted a life of commitment and discipleship like the lives of those I was reading about. So eventually I joined a circle of radical disciples of Jesus Christ where I met and married my husband, Herb, at Reba Place Fellowship in south Evanston, Illinois. Reba Place sent Herb as part of a group of five men to work in the slums of Chicago; it was there in November 1958 that we actually met! I was on a weekend work camp there from Goshen College. And it was there in April 1959 where I first met Mary Klassen, my future mother-in-law, when she came to visit us and meet me. Chicago was also where we moved as newlyweds, to a rat-threatened, ground-floor, windowless apartment—our base for the next year. We both studied at the University of Chicago Divinity School, while working part-time in the needy neighborhood.

Many years would elapse before I would ever set foot on the soil of the country that so fascinated me. Reading a book by the English spiritual leader, Jesse Penn Lewis, with a description of her standing in Red Square, Moscow, I recall hearing an inner voice say, "You will also stand there one day."

*St. Basil's Cathedral in Moscow's Red Square*

At the time it seemed preposterous. Russia was a closed country. And though we in the West did not know the full extent of horrors suffered under Stalin, it was not a place for tourists or missionaries.

From 1965 through the early 1980s, we led a very busy life with our five children in the Fraser Valley of British Columbia, living at first with my widowed mother-in-law, Mary. My husband, Herb, after teaching for a few years at Trinity Junior College, Langley (now Trinity Western University), followed his heart into prison ministry. He served as a chaplain for many years, which involved us moving from Mary's house in Clearbrook to a large farmhouse on the edge of town. There we ran a halfway house for ex-inmates and other needy people. During those years, I was also involved in a national women's ministry, Women's Aglow Fellowship.

Yet it was at this time that our interest in Russia began to deepen. In Mary's house hung a large portrait of her husband, Cornelius or CF. I sensed the unseen influence that this godly man had played in the lives of those around me, and often wondered why no one had ever written a full biography telling about the accomplishments of his very busy life. Herb and I decided we would tackle it as a couple. This involved Herb taking a trip in 1984 to the Mennonite World Conference in Strasbourg to gather material on CF. The book,

*Ambassador to His People: C.F. Klassen and the Russian Mennonite Refugees*, was eventually completed and launched in July 1990 at the following Mennonite World Conference in Winnipeg, Manitoba.

That summer our lives seemed to be at a kind of crossroads. Herb's work at the prison and the halfway house came to an end, as did my work with the women. We were looking for a new challenge that we could work at together. Several of our children were involved in a mission organization called Youth With A Mission (YWAM). Two years earlier, in 1988, we had taken a three-month course with YWAM in Virginia for mature students called Crossroads. That course ended with an evangelistic outreach and the group had headed for the Olympic Games in Seoul, Korea. We decided not to join them. We would wait for an opportunity to go on an outreach to Russia, the land to which our hearts were already drawing us.

The year 1989 came and we were still waiting. We thought often of a prediction we had come across during our research into CF's life, a prediction he had made at the time he left Russia in 1928. In the 1920s, he worked at a place called the Menno Centrum in Moscow, bringing famine relief to the Mennonite villages. The Russian Revolution and civil war had torn these settlements apart. Their people were scattered far and wide. Many fled to new lands in North and South America, as well as distant parts of the Soviet Union like Siberia, Kazahkstan, and Kyrgystan. All religion was repressed and all church bells silenced. The graphic image regularly shown on TV was that of the dynamiting of Moscow's Cathedral of Christ the Savior. The impact of Stalin's order sent the huge bells crashing to the ground. Yet Herb's father, CF, had predicted, "One day the church bells will ring again in Russia. And we will return to minister to our people. Only this time it will be with spiritual not physical bread."

Could we ever be part of that new venture, I wondered? Or could CF have ever dreamed that his youngest son with his English wife would one day return to CF's beloved city of Moscow to seek out some of the Mennonite remnant that still remained in that land?

Waiting and uncertain, I took a writing course at Regent College in Vancouver with Madeleine L'Engle during the summer of 1990. She encouraged us to write a sonnet. Reflecting on CF's prediction and the brutal destruction of the faith and the way of life in the Mennonite settlements, I wrote the following sonnet, sensing that something new was in the air.

> *For half a century no bells were heard,*
> *across the vast expanse of Russia's lands.*
> *The faithful summoned by a nod, a word,*
> *were gathered in, in furtive, secret bands.*
> *Year after year the silent sufferers knelt,*
> *in hidden rooms and far-off prison cells,*
> *their bonds of fellowship more sensed than felt,*
> *their quiet songs replacing joyful bells.*
> *But now a wind is blowing through the land*
> *and from the rubble of the hidden years,*
> *fit tribute to the Father's guarding hand,*
> *a church emerges, washed with martyrs' tears.*
> *And far and wide from steeple, tower, and dome,*
> *the bells ring out, calling God's people home.*

Ms. L'Engle liked the sonnet and even said she hoped I could one day go to Russia.

After the summer course, Regent agreed to allow me to resume studies toward a Master of Divinity, a degree I had begun many years before at the Chicago Divinity School. But I never actively pursued this in light of our growing interest in all things Russian. The future seemed wide open for us. We went to the Mennonite World Conference in Winnipeg and launched our book on CF, even meeting a few Mennonite visitors from Russia.

We also made some inquiries at the Mennonite Central Committee (MCC) as to whether there were any prospects for service in Russia. We were told that, although things were beginning to loosen up somewhat, and though from time to time during the Cold War people were able to visit there and attend meetings or conferences, as yet no one was attempting to take up residence and work full-time there. In fact, no one had officially done that since Herb's father left in 1928. However, MCC promised to keep us in mind in case anything changed.

It was not long afterward, however, that we received our long-awaited invitation to Russia. Art DeFehr, a Mennonite entrepreneur in Winnipeg, was looking for someone to be seconded through MCC to help start an organization encouraging young business leaders in the new climate emerging in Russia. So it was that, in the fall of 1990, we moved to Moscow to begin our five-year MCC assignment. The Soviet Union was beginning to crumble, and that Christmas the church bells in Red Square were rung once again.

*Maureen and Herb Klassen, 1990*

Our first two years in Moscow were occupied with many different things: mastering living in the still Soviet city, facilitating the work of DeFehr's organization for Christian business leaders (SUN, Soviet Union Network), consulting for a Protestant publishing house, and representing MCC in various ministries and relief efforts. To aid in all these activities, we were learning Russian with a tutor who came to our home, mainly in the second year. Managing the shopping lineups and negotiating the huge transportation system of buses, trains, and the famous Metro system was challenging, but we came to love our city and found its bustling life and especially its rich culture enormously stimulating. And above all, we treasured the relationships we were building with the Russian people.

We had already lived in two different apartments before we found the one on Lomonosovsky Avenue where we received Erika's telephone call in 1993. We had been looking for a larger apartment to facilitate the expanding work. This third apartment was close to the new Moscow University in the famous region called Sparrow Hills, across the Moskva River. It was in a solidly built structure, designed to house academics from the university. We leased our apartment from an elderly widower, an award-winning economist now declining in health who needed added revenue to supplement his meager state pension. Its three large rooms served us well for the combined functions of living accommodation and office space for our MCC work.

It was here that, together with our co-workers, Lawrence and LaVerna Klippenstein, we launched what we called the Moscow Mennonite Centre. The large front room with its outlook onto a spacious, leafy square was where we entertained a wide diversity of guests. There were Russians interested in learning about the Russian Mennonite story during these last days of the Soviet Union. Others were hoping to reconnect with their wider Mennonite family in the West. There were also many visitors from abroad. The Mennonite Centre was home to our modest library of books on history and theology, including Barclay's Bible commentaries in Russian and the five-volume *Mennonite Encyclopedia*. Here on a solid wooden table sat our samovar and tea things, at the ready. We held gatherings at the Centre on Sunday afternoons where we discussed many topics including our faith and the history of the Mennonite people in Russia. After London, Moscow was the second Mennonite Centre in which I worked and it again became a key place in my own pilgrimage of discovery.

It was here, three years into our assignment, that Erika's telephone call came that afternoon in 1993. The biography of C.F. Klassen was behind us, but now a different story was emerging. It was the story of Mary's experiences in Moscow during the Russian Revolution nearly eight decades earlier.

# 2

# Mary Martha Brieger

Mary Martha Brieger was born on June 7, 1891, in Riga, Latvia, of German Lutheran stock. Her parents were Louis Christopher Brieger (1852–1910) and Clara Gertrude Goeschel (1862–1917). Riga, an ancient city that once was part of the Hanseatic League of key trading cities, lies on the northern edge of lands subjugated by the mighty Russian Empire, far away from the fruitful plain of Ukraine where Mennonites settled.

She enjoyed a comfortable childhood in Latvia's capital city, Riga. At that time, her family lived a fairly sheltered life, in spite of the uncertain political and economic times in the Russian Empire. Her father was a business man and their home life seems to have been peaceful. There was the added pleasure of the nearby beautiful coastline of sand dunes and pine trees characteristic of the Baltic region, where the children could enjoy frequent times of relaxation during the summer months. Mary was the middle child, between two sisters, Erika and Irmgard. Each had a very different personality. But Mary seems to have been the most assertive. At times she took charge of the others.

They lived on a pleasant family estate, perhaps inherited by her mother, and they had the blessing of a family *dacha* (country retreat or summer house) at the coast nearby. It was there that Mary developed her lifelong love of nature and growing things. It was here too, clearly, that she developed her taste for the Russian concept of dacha life with its commitment to rusticity and simplicity.

Typically, dacha life offered Russians a refreshing change during the summer months from the rigors and demands of their regular life, especially the long, cold winters. Apartment dwellers could enjoy a more relaxed pace in the open countryside at their cottages, and even grow their own produce in their summer gardens. The dacha tradition dates back to Tsarist times and continued right through the communist period. Today, most Russian cities, government departments, and major industries have land allocated for people to build their dachas, a welcome respite from crowded apartment living.

*Brieger family with Mary (far right) in Riga, ca. 1900*

Mary's childhood memories of that period were peaceful ones shared with her sisters. There were beaches near their dacha where Mary's adventurous spirit would allow her to run free. She was a great runner and loved to swim.

Even as an older woman, Mary's energetic character was evident. She would regularly walk the five miles from her house in Clearbrook to nearby Abbotsford, graciously declining the many offers of a lift from passing motorists. Once when she was mounting three flights of stairs in the hospital, she was accosted by a doctor who rebuked her for not using the elevator. She laughingly told him that she had just walked all the way from Clearbrook, five miles away! She loved to roam around her large property on Old Yale Road tending her plants and garden—happy to spend a large part of the day in the fresh air, sharing meals with guests outside or romping with her grandchildren in her garden.

Visualizing her childhood with her two sisters on their estate, I imagine her climbing the great pine trees of the beautiful coastal region where their dacha was located, while their father snoozed on a bench nearby below, supposedly watching over his three daughters. From the heights of those trees, she could have seen the deep blue of the beautiful Baltic Sea nearby reflected in her own blue eyes. She may have wondered whether she would ever cross that sea to visit cities like London or Paris. These were the cities her father visited on his business trips, from which he brought home those colored biscuit tins with pictures of the Queen.

Mary's assertive personality meant that she often found herself in charge of others' lives. It seems that Mary's capacity to "take charge" manifested itself early and carried her through a lifetime of challenging circumstances that would include: helping needy would-be emigrants in Moscow, taking care of banking responsibilities for raising the *Reiseschuld* (Mennonite travel debt owed to the Canadian Pacific Railway or CPR) after coming to Canada, and solo parenting her family in Winnipeg.

Her tenacity was also evident when she undertook the challenge of moving the family from Winnipeg to Abbotsford in 1948, while her husband was away helping the Russian Mennonite refugees in Europe. Her quiet, take-charge capacity would be the characteristic that helped her give essential help and protection to her sisters, and even to their families, when they also immigrated to Abbotsford in the post-war years.

As the middle child of the family, Mary's personality seems to have been very different from what we know of her two sisters. In spite of her good looks and attention to detail in appearance, she was never vain; and at least in her later life, she was never one to enjoy shopping for clothes. In fact, in those years, she had two dresses, hand knit by herself. These, she declared, would do her for the rest of her life! Her favorite dress was the dark green one, which she always referred to as her *grünes Kleidchen* (little green dress).

Mary had a great love for literature and, from childhood, was fluent in several languages. She could recite long passages not only in her native tongue of German, from Goethe and Schiller, but also from eminent Russian poets like Pushkin and Lermontov. What she had learned in her school days came back to her many years later. I recall her relating, laughingly, how she impressed leaders of the church like the eminent C.C. Peters when he visited them in Canada—she recited long passages from these writers, passages that they had both learned in their Russian education.

Mary and her sisters received an excellent education in Riga in the early years of the twentieth century. The long and colorful history of the Baltic nations made for a rich cultural mixture, reaching back to the days of the Teutonic knights and blending strains of German and European traditions with the more recent domination of all things Russian. The girls attended a private German school for girls in the city with the imposing name: *Fräulein Adelheid von Wierehns Töchterschule von dem Höchster Ordnung* (Miss Adeleid von Wierehn's Girls' School of the Highest Order). She later loved to pronounce the pompous-sounding name of her school with a laugh! Here they were nurtured in all the niceties of German culture appropriate to young ladies, in preparation for comfortable lives as wives and mothers. The German Lutheran tradition and its catechism were a crucial part of the curriculum and Mary grew up knowing much of the latter by heart.

Mary was apparently very gifted at drama during this part of her life as a school girl. She memorized not only her own part in plays the students performed but that of the rest of the cast, filling in whenever there were lapses of memory!

I imagine the young Mary as quite an outspoken woman. Sometimes this could be viewed as cheekiness in a young child. But the woman I came to know as my mother-in-law, often rather frank and direct, could always find ways to state things graciously and to deal honestly with other people. It was clear that she was no respecter of persons. She was compassionate to those whom she met, regardless of their lot in life. But she was no one's fool; she did not allow herself to be manipulated by anyone. She usually got the last word and the last laugh. One of her favorite quotes, often still heard in our family to this day, could excuse anyone's eccentricities: *Jeder geht verrückt auf seiner eigenen Art* (everyone goes crazy in his own particular way).

The spiritual nurture Mary received as a child was somewhat different than what she would have experienced in a Mennonite home. The formal religious scene of the large German Lutheran Church in the city likely gave her a framework of faith without the vital personal dynamic Mary was to seek later in her life. It took many years for her personal relationship with her Savior to flourish. We do know, however, that she was confirmed as a young girl, in the Lutheran church in Riga. This is evidenced by the hymnbook still in the family, inscribed with her name, the date, May 31, 1909, and two Scripture verses: John 18:37 ("Everyone who belongs to the truth, listens to my voice") and Revelation 2:10 ("Be faithful unto death, and I will give you the crown of life").

Her innate sense of justice, her humor, and her zest for living marked her from her youth. I sensed in her a longing for a church that truly practiced what it preached and distinguished itself in acts of mercy and compassion, a longing I shared also. The family attended the famous Lutheran cathedral of the city, but we have no real understanding of the role that faith had in their daily life as a family—a contrast to the life of a Mennonite village where the faith of its inhabitants threaded through every aspect of their lives from the field to the school, and from the church to the kitchen table. Mary would doubtless have been struck by the immediacy of Mennonite piety when she met Jakob J. Reimer, her first husband, and eventually visited his native village of Karassan in Crimea several years later.

Mary seems to have been the musical one in her family, continuing with her piano playing all her life. We still have the volumes of classical music, as well as collections of Russian songs which she brought with her from Russia, now carefully re-covered in protective thick paper. In the latter collections is the plaintive Lermontov song about a traveler stepping out alone onto a lonely highway; it constantly runs through my mind as I recall Mary's living room with its baby grand piano in the corner overlooking the acacia trees of her Clearbrook home. And I can still recall her voice singing the words in Russian, a language then strange to me, but one I later came to love.

Mary excelled at needlework, and never ceased at it all her long life! When her children were young, she crocheted little dresses for her twin girls and knitted sweaters for her boys, even adding one to match for Victor, the son of CF and Mary's dear friend, F.C. Thiessen. Later she began more elaborate works. Her hands were never idle, especially on those many occasions, after they came to Canada, when she sat and listened to stories of other peoples' lives and to reports of their trials and tribulations, not to mention the many long discussions she sat through with visiting church leaders in the busy home she shared with her husband in Winnipeg. She made blankets and cushion covers, and stitched intricate rugs and carpets for walls or floors to keep out the cold of the long Manitoba nights. She gave her handiwork away generously throughout her life, or even, when necessary, sold some in order to finance some worthy project. Some of her handiwork remains in our family to this day. One piece is especially treasured by Susie Doerksen, one of Mary's young friends living in Yarrow, British Columbia.

## My First Meeting With Mary

I first met Mary Brieger Klassen in 1959, when she took the long train journey from British Columbia to Chicago, where her son, Herb, my fiancé, was working in the inner city mission I have mentioned. This enterprising widow had also come to meet me, since her son and I were hoping to be married later that year. She had applied for a free pass from the Canadian Pacific Railway (for which her husband had worked collecting the repayment of the Mennonite travel debt) to take the long trip alone across the continent. I was impressed with her initiative! If she was shocked at the setting in which Herb lived and worked, in a neighborhood dubbed the worst slum in North America, she registered nothing. Nor did she complain about having to share sleeping quarters with me in the home of a fellow worker and his family right in the area. I only remember her warmth and energetic personality. My curiosity was aroused.

*Mary visiting Herb and Maureen in Chicago, 1959*

I was just beginning to learn about my future mother-in-law. Herb had told me a little about the long periods his mother had cared for their family alone in Canada, while their father was away helping

Mennonite refugees in Europe. I was aware of the strong family bond she had preserved with her children and admired her lively personality. She seemed able to make light of any discomfort and adversity!

There is no doubt that Mary always had a great admiration for the vibrant faith and sincere devotion of the Mennonites, even if she could sometimes register some amusement at aspects of their piety that seemed a little strange to her. Yet her lifelong unstinting dedication to the work to which her husband felt called, earned her the gratitude and admiration of humble folk and church leadership alike. Mary always trusted in the overarching grace of God, whose hand of mercy was present in all circumstances. She had a deep sense that her life and the lives of those she loved were in the hands of a faithful Creator who would work things out for the best. Such conviction is clearly seen in her letters—which I include later in the story—written during a time of great suffering and hardship in the midst of the years of the Revolution in Moscow.

The next time I met Mary was on our honeymoon trip to British Columbia in autumn 1959. We stayed two weeks with her in her so-called "glasshouse" on a hill at the edge of Clearbrook, not far from Abbotsford, overlooking a pastoral scene of pine trees and grazing sheep. This was my first glimpse of the way of life lived by this unconventional woman.

The house had been built by Herb according to her wishes shortly after the death of her husband in 1954. It had an unusual design and resembled more a mountain chalet than a conventional house. Its single story had two walls of glass, a tall brick fireplace, and an attic balcony overlooking the living area. It was elegantly furnished, including a grand piano on which she played us Russian folk songs, and an old gramophone on which she played us vintage 78s like Achsel Schutz singing Schumann's song cycle *Dichterliebe* (A Poet's Love). She served me tea in dainty English bone china teacups, and fed us on hearty soups and Russian cabbage rolls.

The garden surrounding the house was colorful and rambling, more like some I'd known in England than the neat row-on-row of vegetables in most Mennonite gardens. A huge lilac hedge bordered the property, which in future years would waft its heady fragrance up to the large sunny deck where she would sit surveying the peaceful sheep field beyond. Around the lawn in front of the house was an assortment of trees and shrubs: a chestnut tree planted from a nut from Frankfurt, and numerous acacias with their beautiful summer profusion of sweet white blossoms, which I later came to love in Ukraine and Crimea.

*Mary's "glasshouse" on Old Yale Road*

A so-called "chicken barn" (which had never seen a chicken!) proved to have been imaginatively organized to serve as our "honeymoon cottage." The overall style was a mixture unfamiliar to my suburban upbringing in London. Years later I came to recognize the Russian attachment to the romantic rusticity of dacha life replicated in Mary's happy life on Old Yale Road, not to mention her lifelong love for the smell of lilacs and acacias and the memories they evoked.

In the farthest corner of her property she had an outhouse constructed. While her house did contain conventional plumbing, Mary favored such features of dacha life. She adorned the outhouse walls with pictures and even one of her embroidery pieces boldly stating, "The Lord will not leave thee, nor forsake thee"—a little touch of her wry humor!

At the time of our honeymoon visit, this widow, bereaved for five years, had been working for some time as a receptionist for a local

Dutch physician, Dr. Jan Buirs. He valued her great language skills (Russian, German, and English), but more importantly, her considerable social graces in handling the local population. She recounted good-natured stories about many of the doctor's patients, particularly their attempts to adapt to Western medical treatments after their very different experiences in Russia. During our short visit in her home, we talked of many things. She was interested in my family and eager to meet them, a wish that was granted in subsequent years. Yet she talked little of her past experiences in Russia.

Looking back on that visit, I realize that my understanding of Mary Brieger Klassen was in part constructed by observing her life and interests, her tastes and convictions. In my years as daughter-in-law of this remarkable woman, I came to know and love her independent spirit and energetic approach to living.

While our two lives were very different, I also felt a growing bond with my mother-in-law and our similar circumstances. My involvement with the people called Mennonites was also unusual; and we were both "Gentile brides" coming from different ethnic backgrounds, something Mary and I used to joke about. Beyond this obvious bond, I found we had other things in common, too.

Recalling my own childhood, I shared an affinity with her upbringing and tomboy tendencies, climbing trees and exploring local woodlands. I also remember being told that I was "too bossy." But then, in later life, such qualities stood me in good stead when I served as head-girl of my high school, as team leader of the volunteer work camp for international students during my university days, and as parent of a large household in Canada.

Another thing we shared was our love of drama. I also attended a girls' school where we performed one of Shakespeare's plays every year. It was a great privilege to be granted a role in each of these plays while growing up. The challenge of learning and remembering the lines is often relived in my dreams to this day. But my memory wasn't as good as Mary's!

The ancient city of Riga, which offered the Brieger sisters a rich culture of the arts, including concerts, opera, theatres, and art galleries, reminds me of my own youth in the city of London. My mother took great pains to bring my sister and me to such places of artistic culture in our youth, even during the dark days of the war. I have treasured such enrichments to a young girl's life my whole life; and they were one of the many ways that I felt Mary and I shared a kindred spirit.

One thing, however, that we did not have in common was needlework! I seemed to be all thumbs as a child when it came to sewing. I preferred drawing and painting, and even considered that as a career until literature claimed me.

As I gradually learned more about her role as wife to the well-known CF and mother to her five children, never was there any allusion to the chapter of her life that was left behind in Russia. Nor was I ever told that her very public role as wife to CF had been preceded by a broken marriage in the turbulent years of the Revolution. Perhaps this was due to the stigma of divorce that was prevalent in Mennonite circles in those years or maybe to her strong desire to protect her family.

As we began the long drive back to Chicago after our honeymoon, I was carried by the very pleasant memories of our stay with Mary and her family. I had met Herb's oldest brother, Harold, for the first time, along with his wife, Ruth, and their children. Herb's other brother, Walfried, had attended our wedding in Chicago with his wife, Helene, and some of their children. I had only missed Irmgard as she was away teaching in India. Still, the idyllic life in the Fraser Valley among thousands of other Mennonites seemed like a rather irrelevant oasis, when one considered all the needs of the world, not only in North America but around the globe. I remember thinking it was the last place I'd ever want to settle. How we have to learn to be careful what we promise ourselves!

Five years intervened before I met Mary again. These years were spent in England. After completing our studies at Chicago Divinity School, we decided to go to England for a period, since Herb had never met my parents and I was expecting our first child. Somehow, I didn't fancy giving birth in the rundown west side of Chicago where we had been living that year.

We arrived in England in the spring of 1960, just in time to welcome our firstborn, Tanya, in August of that year. Herb met my parents for the first time and we were able to stay with them for several months in the home where I had been born. Following this, we lived for a few months at the London Mennonite Centre, where I had first encountered Mennonites a few years earlier.

Through contacts given us from Reba Place Fellowship, we then pursued a very meaningful relationship with Quakers for five years. A renewal movement among English Quakers called The Call Group had heard of the renewal happening among Mennonites in America and had extended an invitation for direct contact. It was enriching to fellowship with another historic peace church during our time living among them in the British city of Gloucester.

It was while living among the Quakers in Gloucester that we first heard of the new movement of the Holy Spirit in the Anglican Church. Through our contact with Michael Harper, a curate then at All Souls Langham Place in London, we experienced a deep renewal in our faith. It had always been clear to me that Anabaptism was also a movement of the Spirit, especially in the writings of men like Hans Denck.

*Irmy, Margaret Harvey (holding Tanya), Maureen, and Herb in England, 1960*

Our involvement with this contemporary renewal movement led to my request for water baptism. No one had suggested this to me before that time, and I had been warmly welcomed as a true Anabaptist! So in the waters of the Severn River nearby, I became one in fact. The deepening of our faith gave us a desire to share our experience with Herb's Mennonite friends back in Canada, whom we had heard were also being touched at that time by the Holy Spirit movement.

During these years, Herb was able to obtain teaching jobs in British high schools. He taught Religion and even Latin. As our family increased to include two more children, sons Matthew and Stephen, we sent many photographs home to family in Canada and received many letters from Herb's mother, always a prolific letter writer.

In 1965, after a five-year sojourn in England, we began to receive news that Mary was showing early signs of Parkinson's disease. We decided that it was time for us to return home to Canada. Mary's letters mentioned nothing about her own health, but did express her keen desire that we come back to Canada.

We moved to British Columbia in October 1965 and Mary opened her home to us. Now that we were a family of five, quarters were obviously cramped and this time it was Mary who set up house in the chicken barn/honeymoon cottage! But we essentially lived and ate together as a family. With winter approaching, better accommodations were clearly needed. But she wanted to keep us under her wing, so she began to look for ways to facilitate us remaining as a household. Providentially, in her view, at that moment a neighbor wished to remove a small cabin from his property across the street. For a nominal sum, the cabin was moved to Mary's property and we began to renovate it to house our small family of five; and so that we could move Mary from the chicken barn back into her own residence.

We felt like real pioneers in our little cabin with its cozy woodstove and simple furnishings, many contributed by Mary and other friends and family. She helped us all she could to adjust to life in Canada and we shared a common life as a family, as far as our various jobs and responsibilities allowed—Herb taught at Trinity Junior College and I taught music part-time at a local Christian Reformed school. I sometimes felt the simple life we lived in that cabin might be similar to life in a village in Russia, and even then wondered if that might ever become a reality.

On Sundays, Mary would join our carload on the way to church, wearing her signature elegant dress, fashionable shoes, and one of her many hats, always clutching her purse and large Bible. She made sure she attended her favorite adult Sunday school class, which she said she enjoyed more than the formal church service, since it allowed her to participate with the occasional insight and opinion!

Our pleasant housing arrangement lasted for a year or two. But when I became pregnant with our fourth child, Mary decided she should move us out of the tiny cabin into her house. The cabin, she decided, was very adequate for one person and had plenty of room to entertain her many guests. One morning she announced her decision in her characteristic dramatic style by arriving on the deck of our tiny home, dragging her bedding and declaring that the time had come for the switch.

Mary lived happily in the cabin for several years. She even hosted my parents from England in 1967, when they came to meet their new grandson, our son Mark. Mary was a most gracious hostess, one who enjoyed meeting new people. She and my mother continued to correspond after my parents returned to England. Herb enlarged the main house for our family and a new baby, Rebecca, in 1970. This enabled us to live harmoniously beside Mary with regular daily contact.

Our children grew up enjoying their grandmother and she in turn enjoyed their visits. Our little son, Stevie, would bring her his favorite book, *Lucy Mouse*, for her to read to him. We often ate together and shared our various visitors with one another. One regular visitor was a local widow, a Russian woman who had married a Mennonite. Mary enjoyed talking Russian with her over their tea and our children found listening in to this strange-sounding language fascinating.

Mary was taken from us in 1971, the year of her stroke; although she only actually died five years later in 1976. On the day of her stroke, I had a bad migraine headache. She came to see me early that morning. She pitied me struggling to care for my children with such a pain and declared that she wished she could take the pain for me. I didn't see her that day or the next. When I had recovered and we went to check up on her, she was lying prostrate, unable to speak clearly. Herb accompanied her in the ambulance to the hospital; and despite her incapacity, she tried to quote to him this verse from von Zinzendorf's German hymn that she remembered from her childhood:

> *Christi Blut und Gerechtigkeit,*
> *Das ist mein Schmuck und Ehrenkleid;*
> *Damit will ich vor Gott bestehen,*
> *Wenn ich zum Himmel werd' eingehen.*

> (Jesus, your blood and righteousness,
> My beauty are, my glorious dress;
> In these I'll stand before your throne,
> When I at last reach heaven's home.)

The rest of her years were spent in the Menno Hospital in Abbotsford where her daughter, Irmy, gave her especially fond care.

When Mary finally lost her speech completely, I'm not sure whose loss was the greatest—Mary who lost her power to communicate to us or we who lost her stories and the answers to the many questions we had never asked her. With her, died the secrets she chose not to divulge and a whole chapter of her life she no doubt believed would remain forever hidden.

In time, providence allowed us to discover some of those secrets and to open a small window onto that hidden chapter.

Mary would have never dreamed that we would one day meet Erika, the daughter of her first husband, Jakob; or that we would learn from Erika more about the hidden years that Mary and Jakob shared in Moscow. She also had no idea that some of the questions her son, Harold, carried in his heart for a lifetime, would finally be answered by that simple telephone call to his brother in Moscow so many years later.

# 3

# Discoveries

Erika Reimer Gurieva had known all her life that she had a half-brother somewhere in Canada. Harold Klassen, Herb's oldest brother, was sixteen before he found out that he wasn't CF's son. And he certainly never dreamed that at the ripe age of nearly seventy he would discover an unknown half-sister.

The only clue to these facts, and to the questions that had hung over the Klassen family for a long time, happened in Winnipeg on Harold's sixteenth birthday, October 5, 1939. Though I had been told of this event by other family members, I little realized the part Herb and I would have in exploring its fuller significance many years later. While it happened many years after the critical period in Moscow that we want to explore in this narrative, it captures a moment in time that gives us an insight into relationships that would significantly affect members of our family past, present, and future. I have reconstructed the event as faithfully as I can.

If we move forward from the scenes of happy girlhood, Mary, the middle sister, has become a mother and has sailed across the ocean to a new home in Canada. She is now part of a young family; they are enjoying the life of freedom as immigrants in the city of Winnipeg. Theirs seems to be a happy family—she and her husband, CF, and her children: Harold, her firstborn, then Walfried, Herb, and one daughter, Irmy, whose twin sister, Tinalie, died at the age of two and a half. It is the year 1939, ten years after their arrival in Canada.

C.F. Klassen has been busy for over a decade collecting the repayment of the *Reiseschuld* (travel debt) from the 21,000 Mennonites who have come to Canada to escape the forced collectivization of their farm lands and the loss of religious freedoms that were part of the post-Revolution Soviet program. The years have not been easy for them, but they are all grateful for their freedom to pursue life and their faith. CF takes pride in his sons and daughter, their activities and gifts.

It is early evening at the Klassen home on Harold's sixteenth birthday. Mary is clearing away the special birthday supper they have just enjoyed. CF has withdrawn to his study and Harold has gone up to his room to try out the new fountain pen he has just received for his birthday. His brothers are playing a noisy game in the next room. Suddenly, Irmy breaks in, "Papa wants to see you in his study, Harold." He gives her a questioning look, before she continues, "Yes, now! Come on!"

*Harold Klassen at sixteen, 1939*

Harold descends the stairs slowly. Has he done something wrong? But hardly, this is his birthday. His curiosity is aroused.

CF turns to welcome him with a reassuring smile. "Come on in. Sit down. Run along Irmy." She reluctantly complies.

Harold takes one of the upright chairs along the wall of the study, which is mostly occupied by his father's huge desk. One chair remains near the door, and suddenly, Mary slips in from the kitchen. She is still removing her apron, folding it with uncharacteristically nervous movements. Harold picks up a little of her anxiety and searches his father's face for clues. His mother's usual lighthearted banter is missing, so he waits for his father to break the silence.

"Harold," he begins, "have you ever felt that I have treated you in any way differently from your brothers?"

"Well, no. I mean, of course not!" The boy is bewildered. He searches his memory. Why would his father ever think that? Has he ever complained? He glances at his mother. She tries a smile, but something tense is flickering across her face and she looks away. He is unnerved to see this in her usual self-assured demeanor.

"I have something I want to tell you, Harold," his father continues. "I am not your real father."

*The Klassen brothers: Walfried, Harold, and Herb, 1939*

The silence hangs in the room between them. Again, Mary is unusually quiet. Harold doesn't look at her directly, but looks down, trying to make sense of what his ears have heard, but his mind cannot comprehend. There are no words coming.

CF continues, explaining haltingly, in short abrupt sentences. "Before you were born, Harold, your mother was married to another man. He was your real father. But life was difficult then. He didn't mean to hurt you or your mother. But he couldn't take care of you. He had to go away. He left you both alone in Moscow. I wanted to help your mother. I wanted to take care of you both. That's when we were married. I took you as my own son and we came to Canada."

There is a pause. There should be questions, but the boy cannot frame them. They swirl around in his head. A different father? Why did he leave us? Where did he go? Is he still there? Who am I really? Pain and separation are familiar motifs in Mennonite stories, but they have never been part of his secure family structure. His mind is clouded and he doesn't know how to respond.

His father is looking anxiously at the boy, whose only response is silence. Mary is looking out of the window at the gathering dusk. Nothing need be any different between us, she may be thinking. Harold is her true son and will always be her special firstborn. Yet in some way, nothing will ever be quite the same. Perhaps she wonders if they have done the right thing in deciding to do this on Harold's sixteenth birthday, and how this knowledge will affect his future and his relationship with her.

CF speaks the needed reassurances. "You know that your mother and I truly love you. You are no different to us than the other children. And no matter what anyone will ever say to you, you have nothing to be ashamed of. You have nothing to regret."

Somewhere inside of himself, the boy wants to be hugged. But awkwardness hangs in the room and he leaves without looking either of the adults straight in the eye. He climbs the stairs to his room, feeling the encounter has been cut off abruptly, his many questions left unanswered. As he sits down on the bed it dawns on him. He hasn't even asked his father's name.

Reflecting on that day at the end of his life, Harold only said "There were many tears."

But on that day an important piece of information about his life was imprinted on the young man's mind and heart. The many unanswered questions that this revelation raised, however, would sit with Harold most of his life. It would take the unlikely forging of a link granted to his younger brother, Herb, nearly fifty years later in an apartment in Moscow, the long forsaken city of Harold's birth.

Harold remained a cherished older brother of the family. He did well at his studies, graduating with a degree in electrical engineering. After moving to British Columbia, he taught at Sharon Mennonite School in Yarrow, and later at Mennonite Educational Institute in Abbotsford. Later in life he found work as an employment counselor to be a better fit than teaching. Singing in the church choir was something he always enjoyed. On August 25, 1951, he married his sweetheart, Ruthie Thiessen, daughter of F.C. Thiessen, one of CF's closest friends. Then, in 1956, after the births of his two daughters, Irene and Rita, he was diagnosed with what seemed like an incurable brain tumor. As Mary, his mother, sat beside him in the Abbotsford hospital, she saw his life ebbing away. She alerted the doctors and Harold was rushed by ambulance to Vancouver, where an emergency surgery was done in the middle of the night. It saved his life.

Erika's question, "Is he still alive?" was more significant than she realized.

## Another Discovery, Moscow, April 1993

We now return to that telephone call in Moscow on April 20, 1993, where our story began. Herb's curiosity was aroused as the voice of the unknown woman had inquired, in Russian, about his brother, Harold, and whether he was still living. But it was the quiet assertion that followed that shocked him most, "I am his sister, Erika."

At first, Herb had not known how to respond to such information. He invited her to explain further, and she began to tell her story. "My name is Erika Reimer Gurieva," she said. "My father was a Jakob Reimer."

It was a name Herb had never heard mentioned in his family.

"Jakob Reimer was your mother's first husband," she explained.

Herb knew that his mother had had a prior marriage, before she married CF; and that that union had produced one son, Harold. We had even referred to it briefly in our book, *Ambassador to His People: C.F. Klassen and the Russian Mennonite Refugees*. But we had never heard any more about this man, or of his family in Russia.

Herb had no reason to doubt the veracity of the caller, but we needed time to absorb this interesting new information. He decided to invite Erika to our home so she could share her story with us.

A day or two later, Erika made her way across Moscow on the Metro from her apartment on the northern edge of the city to our apartment close to the new Moscow University. If we had any doubt that Erika's story was true when we heard the beginnings of it on the telephone, our doubts were quickly dispelled when we came face-to-face with the woman who stood on our threshold that afternoon. I saw before me a distinct likeness to our brother, Harold. Slimmer than him and with slighter facial features, there was still an unmistakable resemblance. Like him, she wore spectacles. But her hair, which could by now have been grey, was dyed a deep brown, in the typical Russian style that we had noticed on many women. It was secured at her long neck in a bun. She was neatly dressed and carried a bag containing an album and papers to show us. I was riveted by the resemblance to Harold. Later she joked, "Maureen could not stop staring at me!"

We invited her into the front room where the samovar was ready with tea and the customary Russian cake. And for a long afternoon, we drank tea together and listened to her story. It was intriguing to discover how Erika had found us; we strained to understand her flow of Russian, telling us of the years she had spent searching for her long-lost brother.

"I am the only one left from the Reimer family now," she told us. "My mother died several years ago. My two aunts, my father's sisters, died after many years in exile in Kazakhstan. My Uncle Ivan died a broken man, a few days after he arrived home following his imprisonment in 1947. My father, Jakob Reimer, was arrested in 1937. I never saw him again. We knew he was taken to the Lubyanka prison; and we knew thousands from that prison were shot by Stalin's men. But we were given no information. We were just told that he was dead." Her account was the same as many we had heard.

She went on to tell us about her own family. "My parents were married in Tashkent in 1925. My mother was a Russian musician, a good singer and dancer. My grandmother was from the *Zigeuner* (gypsy) background. My grandfather was a Russian Orthodox priest."

Herb asked, "Did your father call himself a Mennonite?"

Her response surprised us. "What exactly is a Mennonite? Is it something like a Catholic?"

This was not the time to answer this in great detail, though we did give her some literature in Russian about her father's heritage. A deeper understanding would happen gradually over the years that followed.

Then, remembering her childhood before her father was taken, she said, "When I was a child, I always remember a photograph that was hanging on our wall. It was of a boy I did not know. My father said he was my brother, Harold, and that he was living in Canada now, with a family called Klassen. I always wondered if I would ever meet him. My Aunt Sonja told me that for several years she had corresponded with a Katie Klassen, who had been her friend in Moscow."

"That would be my Aunt Katie," interjected Herb. "She married my father's brother, Henry."

"Yes, she talked about my brother, Harold, being with your family. But Aunt Sonja lost track of Katie when the letters stopped coming during Stalin's time. After many years, when things began to get better here in Russia in the 1980s and 1990s, I would often think of Harold; and I decided I would try and find him. I tried many ways. I asked the Canadian Embassy in Moscow if they could trace him. They said there were too many Klassens in Canada! I also tried other agencies, like the International Red Cross. They can connect us with people we lost touch with in those hard years under Stalin. Many left our country then.

But nothing worked for me. Then my husband, Oleg, reminded me that he had relatives in Tel Aviv. He told me that Jews are very good at this kind of thing—maybe one of his relatives could help. It sounded a bit crazy, but I decided to give it a try."

Erika laughed as she related the seeming impossibility of this route, but she decided to go ahead and enlist the help of Oleg's cousin, Erika Oyserman, who was willing to make inquiries at the Canadian Embassy in Israel. It was a long shot; but it worked! Smiling, she reported, "The embassy officials were able to track you down through a connection with a Mennonite Historical Society in Winnipeg!"

Later we learned that the letter had moved through several different agencies, including the Eastern European branch of the Manitoba Genealogical Society, the Winnipeg City Clerk's Department, and the Mennonite Heritage Centre in Winnipeg, where it had finally been received by a Peter H. Rempel. He was replacing the archivist, Lawrence Klippenstein, who was on a leave of absence to work alongside us in Moscow! Rempel had discovered that we were in Moscow and obtained our address from some cousins living in Winnipeg. He sent a note to Harold in Abbotsford informing him that a relative was seeking him, but without details of the identity of the person. By this time Erika had received our contact information in Moscow through Oleg's cousin in Tel Aviv.

"I was so surprised," Erika continued, "when they sent me the information that my brother, Harold, was still alive and living in Abbotsford, British Columbia, Canada. But what shocked me most was to hear that he had a brother, Herbert Klassen, who was at this moment working here in my own city of Moscow! I couldn't believe my good fortune! Here in Moscow!"

Then Erika related a strange glitch. She was given our telephone number, but it didn't work. Then she realized that since she had heard that we were working near the university, she recognized that the area code was wrong.

"I attended this university and I knew it was the wrong code," she laughed. So she tried the right one, and finally connected with us. It had taken one last twist of her ingenuity to forge the final link!

At this point in the story we realized there would be another hurdle to communication. Erika spoke no English, and Harold spoke no Russian. It was here that the providential nature of our presence in Moscow became a factor. We realized that without our interpretive function, there could be no communication between Erika and her newfound brother. But first we needed to learn more ourselves.

The afternoon of her visit, she brought with her the family album that would lay before us the evidence of what she was relating—the photographs from the hidden years of Mary's life in Russia, and Harold's early years.

## The Album

Erika turned the pages of the album and came to a picture of Jakob and Mary. It was as if we had stepped into another world! There is the face of a youthful Mary, looking out at us from another family. She is in the company of her first love, rather than as we had come to know her, standing tall beside C.F. Klassen, so well-known in Mennonite circles. It was somewhat disturbing.

*Mary and Jakob Reimer, May 22, 1915*

There were many pictures of Erika's father's family, the Reimers. There was the typical Mennonite family portrait, theirs taken in the village of Karassan in Crimea. The mother is a good-looking woman with strong features and a firm mouth. The father is tall and lean. There are four children, two boys and two girls. They are all dressed finely and stand proudly together, reflecting a time before any hardships have intruded on their prosperous life in Crimea.

*Reimer family with Mary and Jakob (second row, far right) in Karassan, 1915*

There was another family group picture taken outside in a garden. It seems to be a special occasion, possibly soon after Jakob and Mary's marriage. Mother Reimer, dressed in black, is seated at the center, arms firmly folded. Older relatives are to her left and right. Father Reimer has a young boy, probably a nephew, at his knees. Behind the mother, Sonja stands tall. Sister Katja sits on a stool at her mother's feet. To Sonja's left the couple Jakob and Mary stand close. Jakob is dressed in some kind of uniform, probably that of the Red Cross medical servicemen for which he was conscripted in the early years of their marriage. Mary has one arm draped around his neck, an unusual gesture in Russian photographs. Brother Ivan is at the other end of the back row. The picture is from the early years of the 1914–1918 war.

There was also a photograph of a picnic in Crimea, showing the family in a forest, seated in the long grass beneath the birch trees. The men are in their shirtsleeves; the women are in high-necked blouses and long skirts. At one edge Mary is seen looking seriously into the camera, but appearing somewhat aloof from the gathered company. Perhaps the camera is held by her fiancé, who is not in the picture. Other family members are in the picture. It is a carefree scene of a peaceful interlude during uncertain times, in the lush green paradise of Crimea, before catastrophe would overtake them and banish their way of life forever.

The photographs of the family members, however, told the most poignant story. "These are my two aunts," Erika explained. "This is *Tyotya* Katja and this is *Tyotya* Sonja. And this is my *Dyadya* Ivan. My father was the eldest."

*Erika's aunts, Katja and Sonja Reimer, with grandmother Reimer (center)*

In one photograph the two girls are seated on either side of their mother. They are dressed in long dark skirts and sailor style blouses with dark collars and cuffs, the kind sometimes seen in pictures of the Russian royal children. The picture is probably from the period immediately before the shocking assassination in 1917 of that other special family, Tsar Nicholas II and his family. The Reimer mother at the center looks very serious, almost stoic in her austere dark dress, with arms folded.

Erika looked fondly at the grandmother she knew. It was painful to look at a later photograph of this woman who lived through the horror of seeing all four of her offspring persecuted by a cruel regime, dying alone in her home village of Karassan, while her daughters were exiled to Kazakhstan, victims of the tragic repression. Erika sighed as she handed us the tiny snapshot. The firm rugged features of her grandmother are still discernible beneath ravages of age and suffering. They seem to say, "I have endured."

*Mary and Jakob Reimer (standing), engagement dinner, December 24, 1914*

We searched the album together for more glimpses of the life Mary had shared with this family for a decade during those momentous years. Erika turned the page and pointed to a photograph showing a lavishly set table with fine decorations and candelabra. At the table are seated Mary's two sisters and Jakob's brother, Ivan. Standing behind them are Mary and Jakob. Erika slipped the photograph out of the album and asked us to translate the German words written on the back. It is dated, December 24, 1914, and inscribed, *Für Mama, Unser Verlobungsabend* (for Mama, our betrothal evening). It is the evening of their engagement dinner. The writing is Jakob's, the only piece of his writing we have ever seen.

Then, turning a page, we saw what could be their wedding picture. A young, almost nervous-looking Mary stands beside her Jakob. He is only slightly taller than she is. Her hair is softer than we are used to seeing in our family pictures, her face decidedly more youthful. He is a handsome young man with a narrow face and long nose. Both are serious, almost anxious as they face the camera. This one is dated May 22, 1915.

We sifted through some loose pictures from an envelope at the back of the album. One tiny photograph caught my attention. It is a picture of a lady's desk. On the wall behind the neatly ordered inkstands and papers, in pride of place, is a photograph of the young couple. On the back of the snapshot of the desk is a note in Mary's hand, in Russian, *Jaschenka, this is my first attempt at photography!*

Perhaps Jakob had given her a camera to record details from her life, like this desk where she wrote to him during the time they were separated from one another.

Erika then excitedly drew our attention to a joyful informal snapshot. "This is my father with my brother, Harold, when he was a baby!"

A happy Jakob is lifting his small son high in his arms. The tiny boy, probably barely a year old, is looking trustingly, if a little apprehensively, down into the face of his daddy. It is the testimony of a relationship. The joyful excitement touched us.

"And this is me with my father," she proudly declared, as she pointed to a rather different photograph of herself as a pretty three- or four-year-old held proudly on her father's right arm, her ear touching his forehead. "It is one of my favorite pictures," she said. It preserved a memory of happy intimacy, long before her father was torn from the small family circle that she enjoyed with him and her mother, and many more years before she discovered the ultimate effects of that brutal severance.

"My father was a good man," she offered as comment. Our own comprehension of the life that was unfolding before us in this album could only evoke assent. I considered the male line of descendants, Harold and my nephew, Randy, both fine men—Jakob must have been such, too. Whatever lay behind the sad chapter of Mary's life, linking her to these pictures could not detract from Erika's affirmation.

*Erika with her father, Jakob Reimer*

Then the inevitable questions began. "Why did my father and your mother separate?" Erika asked.

Of course we had no answer. We knew nothing. It would be a question that Erika continued to ask us for a decade, as she learned more about his life and his relationship to our own family. And it was a question that went deeper than was apparent at first. It represented a quest to somehow see him vindicated in our eyes and in the esteem of those far away in Canada, those who could now claim Jakob Reimer as their rightful grandfather.

It occurred to me that if the photographs of those Canadian offspring were in front of me at that moment, I would begin to trace other likenesses in the faces of Harold's children who grew up next door to me, resemblances to Jacob's fine bones and long nose, the slant of the eyes and the angle of the ears to the head. But perhaps more importantly, I began to consider how many other traits of personality, musical giftedness, and tone of voice may have come down to the present generation from this hitherto unknown forebear.

*Harold with his father, Jakob Reimer*

It was beginning to dawn on us that the threads of this discovery in the complex tapestry of our family might challenge some of the assumptions and long-held judgments that had hung over this chapter of Mary's life.

We sensed that a window had opened onto a period of Mary's life that she had kept from us. Were we allowed to look through it? And was it wise to seek more information about a chapter of her life that had remained closed for decades?

What about Jakob? He was once a beloved part of our story. What became of him? How did he fare when the rest of our family fled to the West? Did he suffer under the Soviet regime? Did he perhaps suffer because of his very association with our family? And what became of him in the end? Was he a survivor or a victim of the regime that ruined the lives of so many Mennonites?

*Jakob Reimer*

Erika was beginning to sense the impact her revelations were making. But it was painfully evident that she did not have the answers to many of these questions. As she closed the album, I detected a quiet satisfaction in her face—she has been able to convince us of the bond that now existed between us. She would continue to want answers and would, we discovered, spend many of the following years seeking them. And she would eventually share her discoveries with us.

As she gathered up her album and some of the loose pictures and prepared to leave our apartment, early nightfall had already begun in Moscow. We sensed that this day marked a new relationship, one that would change the remaining time we would spend in that city. How could we bring this sister and her brother together, after a lifetime apart?

## The Klassen Family Photo Wall

It was a shock for us to see the photographs of the matriarch whom we loved and respected taking her place in the album Erika showed us that afternoon in Moscow. The small collection of photographs was scant record of a family's history, with many gaps created by the pain and suffering of the years under Stalin. Mary's part in that history was brief and fleeting.

I could not help comparing that small collection of photographs with the many albums in our own family's possession, as well as the pictures that adorn the special family photo wall in our home. Our photographs are like those of other Canadian Mennonite families from Russia. There are two kinds of photographs: the ones a family carried with them on their journey from Russia, from the days of prosperity before the destruction of the idyllic way of life in the villages, and the ones from the years after their arrival in Canada. The sepia tinted portraits and heavily framed ones are from the former category. Then there are the more relaxed photographs of the years after arrival in the new homeland. For Erika's family, there are none in the second category.

C.F. Klassen was the oldest of thirteen offspring. In the family picture from 1914, he stands tall behind his seated father. His stance seems to presage the shouldering of responsibilities that went far beyond the care of his own mother and siblings, to include the migrations of thousands of his people to new homelands. I am struck by the resemblance of one of my sons to CF. There are traceable likenesses in his sisters to some of our granddaughters, too. Such resemblances have always fascinated me.

Like Jakob's family photographs, the Klassen pictures reveal the comfort and security of rural life in the Mennonite villages. Like all Russian family portraits, even those of the ill-fated Tsar's family, such group pictures are formal and solemn. The parents are usually seated in the center with the children around them. The rigid jaw of the Mennonite patriarch shows his authority and control. Lines of strain on the brow of the matriarch seated beside him hint at her gentler rule. She is the heart of the family, portending the countless women who will survive, sustain, and cherish the next generation, those who will people the albums to come in distant lands like Paraguay, Germany, and Canada. Both Jakob and CF had such mothers who outlived their fathers. CF's came to Canada as an immigrant and had more years to live, surrounded by her family. Jakob's remained in Russia and endured long years of suffering.

*Franz and Justina Klassen family with CF (back row, center), 1914*

A portrait of Mary and CF hangs on our wall beside the wedding picture of the Klassen grandparents. Yet this, the earliest one we have of CF and Mary, is not a wedding picture. In fact, we do not have one of that day. This photograph is of two individual images blended into one frame, yet the edges of each photograph are blurred, denoting that it is a composite picture. I had sometimes wondered why.

Mary brought with her to Canada several pictures of her family. One delightful one shows her sitting with her parents and sisters in a garden. They are seated at a table set for tea with a lace table cloth. It is probably from the school years of her youth, in those untroubled years before the horrendous upheavals that were to follow.

Canada pictures of Mary show her beside CF on happy family occasions. One commemorates their twenty-fifth wedding anniversary. Her hair, already silver, is upswept in her signature style and the usual pearls are at her throat. In another she is wearing the family heirloom, a Russian cameo. There are numerous images of her in their home, always her elegant self among the many relatives and friends of their circle in Winnipeg, and later in British Columbia. It occurred to me that in Erika's album, there were no more photographs of family gatherings after Jakob was torn from their midst in 1937. It was a painful absence.

*Walfried, Herb, Irmy, Mary, and Harold at an orchard in Ontario*

In contrast, my favorite image of Mary in Canada was one with her four children in a Mennonite family orchard in Ontario sometime in the 1940s. They are standing laughing under a profusion of apple blossoms. There is a palpable sense of joy. These family images reflect the happiness of their years in the new homeland after all the years of hardship in Moscow. But these same years were some of the hardest for Jakob's family. Jakob's own whereabouts were unknown, though his family's worst fears remained unsubstantiated. The other siblings were already scattered in exile to forced labor camps, leaving their widowed mother alone. There were no more happy family gatherings.

Hanging on our photo wall is a delightful portrait of Mary's three little boys, the Klassen brothers. Two resemble each other; the third, the oldest, has somewhat different features. I had sometimes wondered why. The revelations coming from Erika's album were beginning to explain.

*The Klassen brothers: Walfried, Herb, and Harold*

If Mary brought any pictures to Canada of the years discovered in Erika's album, they have not come down to us. And the one that is absent from all our family records is the one that so arrested our attention in Moscow. It is the one that now stands on my desk as inspiration for this book: Mary and Jakob's wedding picture.

# 4

# Harold and Erika's Correspondence

After Erika left our apartment, Herb wrote to Harold that same day, recounting many of the details mentioned in our visit with Erika.[2] What would it mean for these two people, now nearing their seventies, to discover a new relationship as brother and sister? It was a warm, brother to brother sharing, but even at that moment, Harold was dealing with his own shock—the discovery of a new sister and also the discovery of more details about his birth father! A period of correspondence followed; Erika read Harold's English letters with help, and Harold read Erika's letters after Herb translated them from Russian to English.

Ever since that sixteenth birthday in Winnipeg, Harold had lived with the knowledge of his father's shadowy identity, but had never asked or been told anything further, except when sometime in his forties he had been given the name of his father. Later, he shared with us frankly that he had been troubled at the interpretation of his father's character in our book, *Ambassador to His People*. Now, hearing more about him from Erika confirmed his doubts and gave him hope of a more positive description of his birth father. Still, he felt his parents, CF and Mary, had done the right thing by him and he was resolved not to worry "about what we don't know and have no control over."

But being confronted with a new sister was another matter. Ruthie reported that when they first received the news from us, she left the very next day on a choir trip for eleven days. So Harold "had eleven days by himself to read and reread the letter, to think and cry over the whole situation."

She reported that at first he was slow to share the news with others, needing to process it all for himself slowly first. "There were

---

[2] Herb's letter to Harold, dated April 23, 1993, is part of the Mary Brieger Klassen personal papers collection, Centre for Mennonite Brethren Studies, Winnipeg.

just too many years of secrecy to overcome all at once—it will take time. I do hope we can come soon to Russia," she concluded.

In the letter reporting our meeting with Erika, Herb reassuringly gave him details about Erika's personality. He also sensed that Harold's rather shy nature would not find it easy to absorb the new reality. Herb wrote: *She was born in 1926. She is a very friendly lady and there are some similarities to you, Harold; something about the mouth and lower part of the face reminds us of you, as well as something about her stance and her character. Most interesting.*

*Erika studied geology at Moscow University, just across the street from us, and had jobs near Lake Baikal and up north near Murmansk. When she returned to Moscow she taught at a Chemical Institute. She married Oleg Guriev, who is half Jewish. His Jewish father had three sisters, two of whom live in Tel Aviv.*

Herb then described to Harold the convoluted way that this connection—through Oleg's cousin in Tel Aviv, through the Canadian Embassy there, via the Mennonite Heritage Centre in Winnipeg, and finally in a telegram to Erika in Moscow—finally reached us through Erika's telephone call. Harold was amazed at this journey, which he said sounded more like a detective story to him!

Herb went on to describe some of the photographs in the album, which I have already mentioned and which Erika eventually sent to Harold.

One photograph that had really caught Herb's attention was a picture of a choir in Moscow, with writing on the back in CF's handwriting. Herb wrote: *One of the pictures she had from her Aunt Suzanna was of little interest to her because the only one she knew on it was Suzanna, but it was of great interest to us. On the back of it, in Papa's handwriting, is this: Chor der Moskauer Deutschen Gruppe am Pfingstsonntag, 7/VI–25, im Klosterhofe, Bolshaya Lubyanka, Moskau* [choir of the Moscow German Group on Pentecost Sunday, June 7, 1925]. *It is signed, C.F. Klassen.*

*Sitting right in the middle of the photograph, Ruthie, is your father* [the director, F.C. Thiessen, who later became Harold's father-in-law]. *At his shoulder is Katie, your sister. Alvin Miller we also recognize and sitting beside your father is what looks like Nalja Isaak, who played the piano at the North End Church in Winnipeg.*

At the right front of the photograph was Suzanna (Sonja), Jakob Reimer's sister.

*Moscow German choir with Sonja Reimer (front row, far right), 1925*

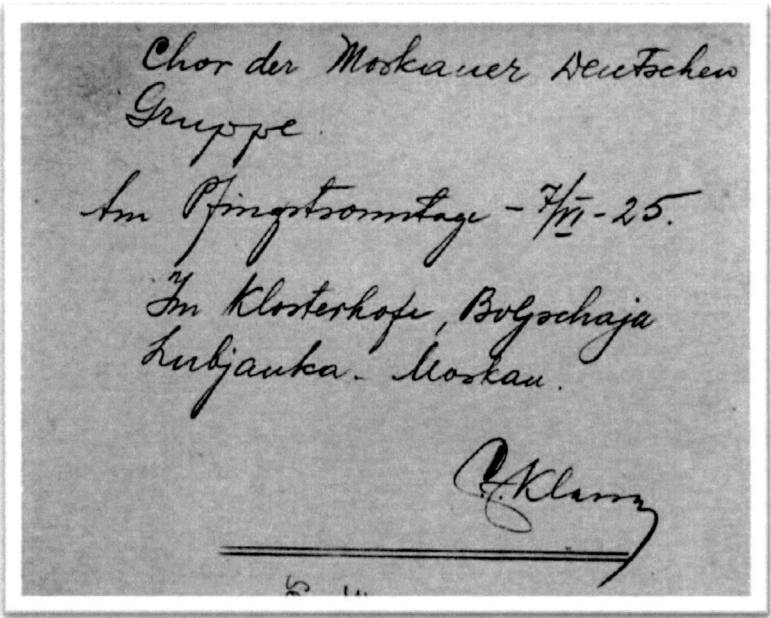

*C.F. Klassen signs the back of the choir photograph, 1925*

## Harold and Erika's Correspondence

It had been striking for Herb to see his father's handwriting in Erika's album. But it would have to await further revelations to understand how close the relationship between CF and Jakob had been.

Herb concluded: *So it has been an exciting day for us. Whether this might be some of the extra push you need to consider making a trip to see us, remains to be seen.*

It's interesting to note that at that time, we knew nothing further about Jakob Reimer, Harold's newly discovered birth father, so most of the focus in Herb's report was on the new sister, Erika. A new relationship had opened up, and seeds were planted for a future visit to Moscow. But this visit would not happen until November. Those few intervening months gave opportunity for the two siblings to begin to get to know one another through correspondence.

The exchange of letters revealed two very different responses to the new realities. For Harold, with a large extended family of siblings, offspring, cousins, uncles, and aunts, Erika was one more additional relative, albeit a unique and fascinating one. For Erika, Harold was the brother she had always longed to meet, and the person from the West to whom she could pour out her heart about all the suffering and deprivation endured under communism.

Harold wrote his first letter to his sister on May 6, 1993; it was warm and friendly.[3]

*Greetings from far away British Columbia!*

*What a surprise . . . what a discovery . . . that I should have a sister in Moscow, who has indeed been looking for me for a long time! It sounds like a dream. Life is indeed stranger than fiction.*

*You and I therefore had common roots: born in the same country, under similar circumstances, children of the same father. My late mother had told me of this latter fact when I was in my forties. But that is where our ways parted. In 1928, I left the USSR with my mother and father and young brother and grew up in Canada. And you remained in Russia. Our knowledge of life in the USSR after 1930 is very limited, but it must have been very difficult for you. I am shocked and saddened that your (our) father was taken from you when you were only twelve. It must have been very difficult for you. It would interest me very much to hear the story of your life.*

Harold continued his letter to her with a brief summary of his own fairly safe and protected life, growing up in Manitoba, going to school and university, and his life in the context of the Mennonite Brethren Church and a warm family.

---

[3] Harold's letter to Erika, dated May 6, 1993, is part of the Mary Brieger Klassen personal papers collection, Centre for Mennonite Brethren Studies, Winnipeg.

*Our family settled in Winnipeg, which has a climate much like Moscow. In 1930, I started school where I soon learned to speak English and was accepted by my new Canadian friends. At home and at church we spoke German, so my Russian was forgotten. I completed high school in 1942 and went on to the University of Manitoba from which I graduated in 1948.*

*When I try to imagine what happened to you during this period of time, it is apparent that our life stories are very different. The land of Russia must have gone through great turmoil and suffering.*

Harold went on to tell her of the move to British Columbia in 1948, his happy marriage to Ruthie, and their family of four, and their five grandchildren. He also mentions that he graduated with an electrical engineering degree, not knowing at that time that his father, Jakob, had also graduated from the same faculty at a German university.

He ended the letter with warm greetings to Erika's family and a request: *Please write and help me to understand all this!*

Harold's invitation was all Erika needed to begin pouring out to her new brother a vivid picture of what her life had been like as the daughter of a man perceived to be an "enemy of the people," something that many in the West, she sensed, did not really understand. She was only too pleased to respond to her brother's request.

On May 21, 1993, Erika began her first letter to her brother[4] in Canada saying: *I was very glad to know that on the other side of the planet I have a brother.* After this, Erika always referred to him as her brother, not half-brother or step-brother.

Immediately she wrote about that picture, which she said her father had hanging on the wall beside his table, the image which stayed with her all her life. *You are sitting on a round stool, dressed in a sailor suit with white shoes. But that I should receive a letter from you and be able to write to you is something I never dreamt possible. You are right; life is amazing!*

Erika then proceeded to tell the story of her father's short life and the tragic circumstances of his family. Her words opened a window for us onto the hardship of so many in the wider Mennonite community who remained behind after their relatives left Russia.

*I want to write to you about the tragic fate of our father. He was a native of Crimea, from a village called Karassan (railway station Kurman-Kemelki). He was born in 1891. His father, your grandfather, was also called Jakob and his mother was Yekaterina Korneevna. There were four children: Jakob, Ivan, Yekaterina, and Suzanna, born in 1900. I called them Aunt Katja and Aunt Sonja.*

---

[4] Erika's letter to Harold, dated May 21, 1993, with English translation, is part of the Mary Brieger Klassen personal papers collection, Centre for Mennonite Brethren Studies, Winnipeg.

*Our father was an electrical engineer. He studied in Germany. Where and when he met your mother I do not know. I only know that at the beginning of 1925 he came to Bukhara, Uzbekistan to build a hydroelectric plant. There he met my mother who worked as a secretary in the central control office.*

*My mother, Vera Protopopova, was a native of the Urals, in the city of Miass, from a family of Orthodox spirituality. Her father was a local priest and teacher, and died when she was about ten years old. I was born in Bukhara on September 6, 1926.*

*Katja Reimer*

Then Erika mentioned something that she rarely if ever referred to: when she was one year old, her family visited the Urals and her grandmother of Orthodox faith had her baptized into the Russian Orthodox Church. Erika may have viewed this as an empty ritual as she grew up in atheistic Russia, but it might explain her return to that faith tradition in her later years.

Her letter continued with a comment to her brother: *Our faith differs from yours, Harold, but God is one.*

Erika then told of her family's life in Central Asia, with a move first to Samarkand, and then to Tashkent, before moving back to Moscow in 1931. At that time all Soviet citizens received passports, which were like resident permits. However, for some reason, Jakob could not obtain one, though her mother did. Was he already a *persona non grata*? So his life as a fugitive began. He had to always search for work and live where he could, thus often separated from his family.

*Father found work in Yaroslavl, north of Moscow, where he lived in a small low-ceilinged room in one of the guard towers of the ancient monastery there, together with his mother and two sisters. Then he moved to Kostroma in a house where he made by hand all the furniture, and where mother and I visited him in the summertime. In 1934, he got work in a Gramophone record factory in Aprilevsk, one hour and fifty minutes from Moscow where he lived again with his mother and two sisters. Katja worked in the factory as a bookkeeper, and Aunt Sonja taught school in Moscow. She was such a good teacher that she was offered a job teaching the children of Kamenev (in Stalin's circle), but after being interviewed she turned the job down. She said Kamenev's wife treated her like a slave! Father was in charge of the whole electrical system of the factory. He visited us two or three times a week, but in the summer, we lived with him there in Aprilevsk. Now it is a city; but then it was a village with a lovely river and a forest.*

After invoking these memories of childhood, Erika embarked on the saddest part of her story, recalling the fate of her grandmother. All four of her grandmother's children suffered so much at the hands of Stalin's merciless regime. She wrote: *Uncle Ivan was arrested before my father. All his property was confiscated (his house and other things) and his family exiled from Tashkent within 24 hours. They tried to come to Moscow, but couldn't live there without the necessary permission.*

She described how the family was scattered in different places, ending up in Siberia and spending the war years there, while her cousin Yuri was conscripted into the army. Ivan eventually returned to them in 1947, after his decade of imprisonment. She wrote: *He had no teeth and several broken ribs, and soon died.*

Erika continued: *Father was arrested on September 4, 1937. It was two days before my eleventh birthday. I remember it perfectly. I awoke early at daybreak. I was sitting on the side of the bed during all the trouble. Our eyes were fixed on them* [NKVD officials, Russian acronym for The People's Commissariat for Internal Affairs] *as they did the search, even leafing through all the books on the shelves. When they were leaving, my father took a rubber ball out of his pocket and gave it to me and told us that it was a misunderstanding and that he would soon return. The higher court will take up my case, he said.*

*But we never saw him again. I waited expectantly for him for many years. He remains in my memory as a very orderly, honest man, and a good craftsman. He taught me to read, to love living things. He was very musical. He played Beethoven from memory and sang in a good tenor voice. He made a dollhouse for me out of plywood, with all the furniture handmade by him. It stood on the windowsill on our second story apartment and I sat on a chair in front of it and played for hours. He also made himself a radio, on which he said he got South America! He was also interested in photography, and I used to like sitting with him in the dark room as he developed the photographs.*

*Sonja Reimer*

*His last gift to me was a book by Alfred Brema,* The Lives of Living Things. *This book is still precious to me. All I have left of Papa's things are a pocket knife, a little crystal statue, and an autograph book. I cherish them.*

*After father's arrest mama was always afraid that she and I would be arrested, too. She lost her job and when the war started she was always afraid that German families would be exiled. In fact, our Aunts Katja and Sonja were exiled to Kazakhstan, without any court appearance. They had to live there apart, because they were not even allowed to live together.*

*In summer of 1950, I wanted to visit Aunt Katja there. I was returning from a geological course and I had asked her to meet me from the train. I was so shocked at her haggard appearance that I hardly recognized her. They were finally freed* [i.e., to live elsewhere] *in 1953, but they were never able to return to Moscow to live, although they did visit us there in 1964. Then they told us that you, Harold, had undergone an operation. Aunt Sonja said she was corresponding with your mother and her friend Kathie (Mrs. H.F. Klassen), but I never got your address from them.*

*Babushka (grandmother) Reimer*

## Harold and Erika's Correspondence

*In the winter of 1972–1973, I visited them in Karaganda. Aunt Sonja was then a retired and respected teacher. She was given an apartment on the main street of Karaganda, where they lived together. Before they had retired, they had taken their mother, our Babushka, back to Karassan in Crimea where she died soon after. What a horrible tragedy she had lived through—all four of her children had been arrested. All that was left was for her to die!*

*I last saw my Aunt Sonja in the summer of 1977 in Karaganda. Katja had died earlier that year and Sonja was already sick from a serious accident. She had been hit by a car and suffered multiple fractures. We went over some old letters together which she read to me. She said she didn't want them falling into the wrong hands after her death. So I destroyed some of them. Among them were letters from your mother, Harold. Sonja died in November of that year, 1977. Neither of my aunts ever married. They were persecuted and exiled and they suffered in ways that made having a happy family life impossible.*

It was from Sonja that Erika received the album that she had shown us in Moscow.

For Harold there was much to digest from this first direct communication with the sister he never knew had been waiting all these years to get in touch with him. We treasure her record of her family's sufferings as a vital glimpse into how very different their life was from the life then being lived by Harold's other aunts and uncles in Canada.

Erika closed her letter by recounting a dream she had a few years earlier, in which someone told her that her father's son was staying in a hotel in Moscow. She had gone searching for him, wondering whether his name was Reimer or Klassen. And when she awoke, she had determined to try to find him. That dream launched her search that had finally resulted in the telegram from Oleg's cousin in Tel Aviv telling her we were in Moscow!

She promised to write again soon about her own experiences after her father's arrest. Harold's request to tell him more of her experiences as a child under communism gave her an opportunity to share deeply. As the child of a condemned person, Erika herself could so easily have become a victim of one of the harshest aspects of Stalin's repression campaign, the suffering endured by the innocent children of people wrongly convicted by the evil system.

Such children became part of a severely disadvantaged group called the *besprizorniki*. The word literally meant those without all care and protection, utterly lawless. Practically speaking, these outcasts from Soviet society became bands of roving child beggars for whom survival was the only lifestyle they knew. They would terrorize local communities, begging and stealing to survive. They lived in any public place available like railway stations or under the huge heating pipes in some of the cities. Children who were left defenseless after the arrest of their parents often ended up here to escape the equally fearful lot of being put into the infamous state orphanages that had the reputation of poor care and neglect, and sometime starvation, not to mention the enforced atheism of the Soviet system. It is understandable that the parents' worst fear was to contemplate that fate for their offspring.

In her subsequent letter,[5] Erika wrote: *Mama was a first class stenographer and had a good job working for a high-level official in the hydroelectric department of the government. But when my father was arrested, she lost her job and her good salary. Our life became very difficult. She then got a low-paying job in some kind of factory. But she was always afraid that she too would soon be arrested. Often it happened this way—the husband was arrested first, and then the wife. Her greatest concern was what would happen to me. She had prepared instructions as to what her sister and her friends would do with me in the case of her arrest, to avoid me being placed in an orphanage. She was always fearful and anxiously preoccupied with this matter.*

*One thing I always remembered was what happened around this time. My mother had a close friend Tanya. They kept in touch daily. Once when Tanya had not heard from us for two days, she became worried. On the evening of the second day, she sent her husband, Paul, to check up on us. At midnight there came a knock on the door. My mother was convinced that the police had come for her! She carefully opened the door and looking down, all she saw was army boots. She collapsed on the floor in a dead faint. When she came to, she could only exclaim; "Why did he have to come so late at night! And in those boots!"*

Then Erika explained that her mother absolutely forbade people to write letters to her; they could only bring them to her in person. This was for fear that letters might be intercepted and used against them, a common practice in such persecutions at that time. There was absolutely no privacy for the individual.

While Jakob Reimer was incarcerated in the Lubyanka, the family was always hoping against hope for his release. Like many others, he had declared his innocence at his arrest, saying that it was a big mistake and that he would soon be returned to them. How many others had clung to that hope in vain! Erika's mother must have realized that there was little hope. But Erika, a young child at the time, always believed her father's words.

---

[5] Erika's letter to Harold, dated August 9, 1993, with English translation, is part of the Mary Brieger Klassen personal papers collection, Centre for Mennonite Brethren Studies, Winnipeg.

## Harold and Erika's Correspondence

*During the autumn after Papa's arrest, my mother took messages for him to the KGB* [Russian acronym for Committee for State Security] *prison and tried to find out more about him. Then suddenly all messages were refused and there were no more answers. Feeling that, out of fear, mother wasn't making enough effort, I went to the Ministry of Internal Affairs* [NKVD] *myself. The queue was long* [she identifies the Moscow streets it stretched along]. *It was winter. I stood for 3 to 4 hours and was freezing cold. A woman took me by the hand and took me to the front of the queue and said, "Let her in; she's freezing!" So they let me up to the entrance of the building. Again I got really cold and another woman took me in a bit further. And so on it went. By the evening I got in to see an official.*

*I remember the big black arm chair I sat in—I felt drowned in it. I remember how my knees shook. I tried to keep them from shaking, but I could not. The official asked me my age and my name and where I was studying. After that he asked me why I had come. I told him everything, He promised to find out all he could about papa, and said he would write to me. Of course he never wrote anything.*

*So we waited. Mama was paralyzed with fear into inactivity, but I couldn't understand this. I was convinced that Papa was innocent and that I should do something. I always believed that he was innocent and that the arrest was a mistake and his release imminent. I should have noticed though that many from the apartment block we lived in were arrested, friends of my mother's at work and friends from my school. I just assumed that they were guilty and arrested legitimately, whereas my own father was innocent. So I was waiting for him to return. He said he would. So we waited until the year 1941. I was sixteen.*

*For us the war began on the night of June 22, 1941. It was a Sunday. Early that morning Aunt Sonja came to us and said, "Don't you know that the war has started?" She knew what this would mean for her and Katja. We turned on the radio and Molotov was speaking. Sure enough the war had begun and in July, Moscow started to be bombed. I remember the hysterical sounds of the sirens. It was especially frightening at night. Mama would urge me to get dressed quickly and go into the bomb shelter. I got dressed and took a big basket and put the cat and some food into it. I wouldn't go without these things. I still have the basket and still treasure it! It's an historic memory!*

*At the end of July, Mama took me to Tashkent with her friend Tanya. We went to stay with her sister, also called Sonja. It was not easy leaving Moscow—the factory, the school, and all the people and places. There were not enough trains for everyone, so people had to travel in freight cars as well. I remember that we traveled with three young geologists. We had upper bunks which were rather inconvenient. Mine ran lengthways along the corridor. One of the geologists offered Tanya her more convenient place. Mama was afraid I would fall out of the bunk and get hurt. One of the geologists told her not to worry, that they would catch me. To which she replied, "By the foot or the neck?" So they offered to put a belt around my waist and secure me to the coat hook. So we traveled for a week together and became quite friendly. They brought me light drinks and took me for walks at the stations.*

*We finally arrived in Tashkent and were met by Aunt Sonja who was very glad we had made it. In Tashkent there were many like us recent arrivals from the danger zones. There were shortages of everything: rooms, food, and clothing. Mother soon got a job with a government department.*

*At age thirty-nine, she couldn't work as a stenographer, because she had lost some of her hearing due to her frazzled nerves. Mother made friends with a carpenter, Vladimir Alexandreevich, and he moved in with us. He was divorced, but had a boy named Orest, Orik at home. He was six years younger than me. In the summer of 1941, he had been staying with his grandmother, Vladimir's mother. Vladimir was conscripted in 1941. When the grandmother died, Orik was left alone so mother took pity on him and brought him into our family. I pitied him, too. Bad enough like me to be without a father. But to be without mother or father must be truly tragic. I went to the apartment where his grandmother had lived, which was now occupied by two old women from Leningrad. I found some old clothes there and made a proper pair of pants and a shirt for him. From a woolen curtain I also made him a jacket. I had learned to make clothes for my dolls, so I was quite good at it.*

*It became more and more difficult to find food. At work mama was given a little garden plot. We planted onions and corn and they grew quite well. So we had corn mash and corn cakes with onions and bread and made out quite well. Orik cried, asking for his usual porridge, but it wasn't available. I had to explain to him that mama was doing the best for him that she could.*

*At mama's work they gave out free vodka on holidays. She would take it and sell it to buy sugar or meat or anything more useful. One day Aunt Sonja decided to bless us by making a soup made from nuts cooked in some kind of oil. It was very tasty, but I've never seen soup like that again! Once Aunt Nina brought us cutlets made from the potato peels that she got at the hospital where she worked.*

Erika then described the grueling regimen she lived under in her teen years in Tashkent. Her routine was similar to many we learned about in Russia. It shocked Harold to learn how different their teenage years had been.

*It was in Tashkent that I began to work at a factory. This meant that I also received a worker's food ration of 800 grams of bread a day, and some other kinds of goods once a month. But soon it was reduced to 600 grams and then to 400. But what was important for me was that I was now transferred from the ordinary school to the factory school where they trained stonemasons for the building trade. It was one of the better schools in Tashkent. But when that course was finished, they sent me to work in the factory for the war effort. So now I had to go to work, and also continue my school studies. I had to get up at 4 A.M. I had to walk 40 minutes to the factory, since public transport wasn't working yet that early. I worked until 5 P.M., had supper, and then headed off to school for the 6 o'clock evening session, studying for four hours until 10 o'clock at night. I was expected to work 8 hours and do 4 hours of school per day, seven days a week. Once a month we got a Sunday off.*

Erika went on to explain that her mother had to help her manage work and school. She also had to protect Erika from the "bandits and hooligans" on the streets of the city and escort her to school across the bridge over the Salor River every morning for fear they would throw her into the river! This life went on for 14 months, through the harsh Tashkent winter, through snow and rain, living in an icy unheated apartment.

*I have never been as cold as this in all my life. My fingers were always numb. But my work kept me going and enabled me to receive supplies. Once I even received material to make a dress and buy a pair of shoes without buckles. I felt like a film star!*

Through such periods of hardship Erika's resourcefulness and perseverance were born. Here too began her persistent efforts to seek justice for her father—if not during his lifetime, then at least for those who would come after him, significantly now for his long-lost son, Harold. As I read about the young girl shivering in the lineup of relatives outside that notorious government office of the NKVD, I saw foreshadowed the woman who later left no stone unturned till she got the information she wanted from the KGB, so many years later.

Erika finished her long letter to Harold on August 10, 1993, the birthday of their father with these words: *Today he would be 102 years old! But he only lived to 45, not even half a life.* She hoped that somehow she and Harold could meet one day in the flesh, though she said she did not expect that she would ever visit Canada. Instead, she would await the arrangements for them to come to visit us in Moscow later that year.

Gradually, Harold would have more opportunity to get to know his new sister over the remaining years of his life. She would share with him about her years at Moscow University studying geology, her marriage to Oleg, a rocket scientist, and their life under the Soviet system. But for now, plans for a trip to Moscow became a priority for Harold and Ruthie, and we encouraged them to be our guests. So it was that in early November 1993, everything fell into place for that memorable visit.

## The Visit to Moscow

Finally it happened that Harold and Ruthie were able to make the journey to Moscow. Harold was eager to meet Erika. And when they stood together that first day in our apartment in Moscow, there could be no doubt that these two were siblings—there were similarities of expression, the set of the jaw and the laugh lines. Each of them wore spectacles. Other similarities only emerged as they spent more time sharing together.

As we sat around our table together there were many questions from both sides. Erika had sent Harold one or two photographs, but now it was time for him, together with Ruthie, to look through the album that had so impacted us that memorable afternoon after Erika's first telephone call. It was riveting to watch Harold look for the first time in his life at photographs of his own father. He was also interested to see photographs of Jakob's family and his parents, Harold's grandparents.

The photograph, however, that he looked longest and most wistfully at was the one of himself as a young child held aloft in his father's arms, joyfully and trustingly. And he would continue to search his heart for any memory of that moment from his all too distant past.

Our conversation that day was considerably slowed by the need for our constant translation. Gradually, the two siblings were able to share some of their common interests and experiences, their education and their family life. Erika was eager to learn all she could about Canada, though she did not dream she would ever be able to visit the home of her newfound brother.

Erika was proud of her native city Moscow, and gratified at Harold and Ruthie's interest in her culture. Ruthie, a keen musician, was eager to attend a concert or two, and Erika was only too willing to secure tickets to some upcoming musical events. She was also happy to show them around the art galleries and museums.

Harold and Ruthie's appreciation of all things Russian pleased Erika. She was glad to take them to some of the best stores for tourists, even though they were places she could never afford to frequent herself. Harold took a special interest in visiting Moscow University, where Erika had trained as a geologist; they even met some of the faculty members there. It was ironic that when Erika managed to make her brother understand that their father had trained as an engineer, Harold was able to communicate the fact that he also had trained as an electrical engineer!

The visit was short, with lots of trips back and forth between her apartment and ours. One day, when the weather was particularly cold and icy, I had determined that we should show our guests Red Square. On our way to Erika's apartment by Metro, we decided to come up into Red Square from the famous underground station, Krasnaya Ploshad, with its brilliant decorations. We viewed the square with its impressive St. Basil's Cathedral and cluster of impressive buildings behind the somber Kremlin walls. But we didn't join the long slow line of people waiting to enter Lenin's tomb just outside those walls. We needed to press on to the warmth of Erika's apartment, away from the biting wind and the snow that was now falling.

We descended again into the Metro station and trouble struck. As we entered the stone staircase, I noticed that ice had already formed on the steps. Suddenly my feet slipped, and I fell down the staircase, grabbing the railing with my arm. It was a scary moment as the crowds of travelers almost trampled me. Herb rushed to help, but I realized that I had seriously wrenched my shoulder.

Somehow we managed to resume our journey to Erika's, where she was awaiting us with a special meal. I remember little of the event due to the excruciating pain I was experiencing. That injury continued to plague me for the remaining period of our time in Moscow. In any case, Harold and Ruthie were able to appreciate the trouble Erika had gone to, creating a special Russian meal with its several courses of soup, meat cutlets, cabbage salad, and chocolate cake. The traditional Russian toasts were also part of the meal and were accepted with courtesy as the host's recognition of their guests' long journey to share this special meal.

Erika was of course very concerned about the plight of my shoulder and provided me with remedies. I would eventually need much help from Russian and Western medical services, including five months of treatment back in Canada. In any case, my condition meant that we were unable to accompany Harold and Ruthie at all the subsequent visits to Erika and Oleg's home. This pushed them to try conversing with Oleg in German. He was a delightful man, a gifted scientist with a once important role in the scientific institute where he worked on rocket research. But he had absolutely no familiarity with matters of faith or religion. Once, when Erika invited Herb to read a portion of the Russian Bible at their table, he was very impressed with the words from the Epistle of John; he asked that they be repeated. To him, their impact was utterly fresh.

Harold and Ruthie's visit included a concert at the great Tchaikovsky Concert Hall, a visit to the Tretyakov Gallery, and a visit to the collection of impressionist art at the Pushkin Museum. Then, toward the end of their time in Moscow, we went all together to the Bolshoi Theater to see a performance of Tchaikovsky's *Iolanta*. Our last minute scramble for tickets meant that we were split up, except for two seats next to each other and near the front. We decided to give those to Harold and Erika.

The story of the opera revolves around a blind daughter and her relationship to her protective father. Late in the story a lover breaks into her life and her sight returns. She is finally able to see those close to her with her own eyes. In a dramatic scene, she and her father meet in a garden, and she sees him for the first time. It was a poignant moment there in the darkened theater as the aria was sung by Iolanta, "Is this really you? Am I seeing you with my own eyes?"

The dramatic irony for these two siblings was palpable. Across the theater we could discern the dim outline of Erika, who was glancing at the long-lost brother seated beside her, so soon to be taken back again to Canada—a brother she had only recently seen for the first time in her life. It was a unique moment granted to us all by the strange miracle of her persistent search for this, her only remaining blood relative on earth. And as I watched them together across the crowded theater, I was deeply grateful.

As I look back on that memorable day of Erika's first visit, when we shared the album, I realized we all faced a kind of watershed of understanding. That day, when Erika had first learned the identity of this mystery woman who had stood beside her father in that album for a lifetime, she had opened a window of discovery that would occupy her for the rest of her life.

We, in turn, had a similar reaction when there, in the middle of a very private record of a family's life in Crimea, so many years before, we saw the matriarch of our own family. For both Erika and ourselves, this new knowledge was beckoning us to a journey of further discovery. She was as ignorant as we were to the later details about her father's life, and what factors had intervened to tear his first marriage apart. It seemed almost unreasonable to expect answers to such questions, but that would not halt the search.

# 5

# Mary and Jakob

Erika entrusted the photograph of Jakob and Mary to our safekeeping, as if she felt their story belonged to our family, too. It was to be shared with the remainder of our extended family in due time. We would eventually need to introduce Harold's children—Irene, Rita, Randy, and Lorri—to the pictures of their rightful grandfather.

As we began to get used to the idea of Mary's life as part of another union, there were many questions in our minds. How did these two meet? What unusual circumstances had brought together a young Mennonite man from the distant Black Sea province of Crimea, with a Baltic German Lutheran woman from the northern land of Latvia? And how was it possible for a time of courtship and marriage to happen in the early years of World War I, and the subsequent years of the bloodiest revolutionary chapter of Russia's history? More importantly, how could we piece together the details of that story from Mary's silence and the very few clues that were now becoming available to us?

At the time of our meeting with Erika, the album was our first introduction to Jakob's life, since Mary had not talked about him in the family. Over the years we have gradually gleaned a little information about his life, though he remains to this day a somewhat shadowy figure. The main details of Jakob's own life came from the biographic outline he was required to give to the KGB at the time of his interrogation in 1937.

## Riga, St. Petersburg, and Moscow (1914–1924)

The ten years of Jakob and Mary's marriage spanned some of the most tumultuous years in Russian history. Their life was defined and circumscribed by war and revolution. After studying engineering in Germany, Jakob went to Riga, Latvia, in 1914, the city where Mary lived. He worked first as a technician at the central power station and later as an electrical engineer for a firm called Mantel and Company. We have learned from Mary's niece, Vera, that he was a friend of another young German engineer, Peter Sadjikoff, who had recently married Mary's sister, Irmgard. He introduced Mary and Jakob, whose growing relationship was overshadowed by the threatening mobilization of the German army and the war that would soon change their lives.

The life of the Brieger family in Riga was already undergoing many changes as a result of the threat of war. Though the family tried to cling to the old ways, changes were in the air and the young women realized the lifestyle of their youth would soon be lost forever. Their father suffered irreversible losses related to the changing economic and political scene. Finances became an urgent matter for the family. Irmgard found work with a local seamstress. Mary's expertise at accounting helped her find work through her father's contacts with a firm called George Malcolm and Sons, with headquarters in Leadenhall Street, London. They offered Mary a job as shipping clerk in their branch office in Riga. She was put in charge of all their foreign correspondence, which made good use of her excellent language skills in English, German, and Russian.

Jakob and Mary's relationship progressed swiftly, something of a whirlwind romance. They were engaged on December 24, 1914, and were married probably on May 22, 1915. Both these events were documented by the photographs in Erika's album. As the German army's eastern front advanced through Prussia, Mantel and Company was evacuated from Riga to St. Petersburg. The city was soon renamed Petrograd by the Tsar to avoid its German-sounding association. Malcolm and Sons also had a branch office in that city. So Mary also moved to Petrograd to continue her work for them there.

For the newlyweds, Petrograd could have been a wonderfully romantic city, with its beautiful architecture, cultural life, art treasures, fragrant parks, and lush gardens. These could be enjoyed in the extraordinary climate of Petrograd's "white nights," given the opportunity they offered for late-night walks along the many picturesque canals. The beautiful St. Isaac's Cathedral dominated the city's skyline. It had been here that, not so long ago, the great writer, Count Leo Tolstoy, had been declared "anathema" because of his criticism of the Russian Orthodox Church.

Mennonites had some affinities with Tolstoy for his teaching on peace and his identification with the peasant masses. As author of the celebrated novel, *War and Peace*, he was a popular author among the general population. In 1910, just a few years earlier, when one of the Red Cross hospital trains paused at the Astapova Station, a group of young Mennonite medical servicemen, like Jakob, stood on the platform, gazing enthralled into the very room where the great writer had just breathed his last.

Mary and Jakob would have had opportunity to enjoy the rich musical culture of the city. There was a circle of fellow Mennonite young people studying and working in the city, including his two progressive sisters, Sonja and Katja. Two photographs of these sisters in the album show two very smart and elegant young women from this period, before the devastating experiences of the Revolution turned their world upside down and dashed the dreams and promise of their student hopes and aspirations. But in the years captured in the photograph, they were beginning to throw themselves into some of the more daring sides of the new movement.

*Katja Reimer as a student, 1919*

There was, however, a downside to life in the newly designated Petrograd, for this was a time of war. The German-speaking circle that welcomed Jakob and Mary was not looked upon favorably. Jakob's musical skills were greatly appreciated by the group, but that did not change the fact that the Germans had now become the enemy. Was that the reason that 1915 found the young couple leaving the city to take the long train journey down to the Crimean peninsula, Jakob's homeland?

Karassan, Jakob's birthplace, was a Mennonite village located in the more fertile central plain of Crimea. During the Crimean War in the 1850s, Mennonites volunteered to serve in the ambulance corps of the Tsar's army, traveling to the front to pick up the wounded. They brought them back to Ukraine on wagons (no railways yet) for refuge and healing at the Mennonite hospitals in the Molochna and Chortitza settlements.

Some of the young men were attracted to the lands they passed through on their journeys. After the Crimean War, when land was getting scarce in Ukraine, some of them ventured forth to establish new villages in these regions in the heartland of Crimea. The climate was attractive and, as long as water was available, the land promised to be a fertile option for their agriculture.

Karassan was one of the first villages to be founded in 1865. By the time Jakob was born in 1891, it was a flourishing community. Lush trees, like mulberry and acacia, and shrubs, like lilac, filled the warm air with their fragrant aroma. Karassan also boasted prosperous farms and thriving institutions, including a fine *Zentralschule* or high school (coeducational after 1910) where Jakob got a good education. C.F. Klassen also attended the Karassan *Zentralschule*, boarding at the home of his Aunt Greta, his father's sister. He became a lifelong friend of Ivan, Jakob's brother. Jakob's sisters may have attended the fine girls' high school in nearby Spat.

Crimea, renowned for its beauty and good climate, was the place that tsars and later communist apparatchiks chose for their palaces and dachas. The earlier settlers were less ambitious, seeking only a modest place to live in peace and pursue their dreams of prosperity. Mennonites loved this setting because it offered a quiet rural existence.

Jakob had been away from his home for several years. He had studied first in Germany, where he obtained an engineering degree at the Thüringer Institute, in the city of Ilmenau. Later he worked, as already mentioned, as an engineer in Riga and Petrograd. It was natural that he wished to bring his young bride home to meet his family, though it seems that Mary had already met his sisters and brother who were also studying in Petrograd. The photograph from the album recording this visit can be accurately dated by the fact that Jakob is wearing the uniform of the ambulance corps. This makes the picture more poignant, knowing that the young couple would soon be separated. Mary has her arm draped affectionately around his neck. How welcoming, we wonder, were the Mennonite people of Karassan to this young woman from Riga? She spoke a different kind of German than they were used to and knew almost no Low German, the popular language of hearth and home in the Mennonite villages. But her warm, friendly disposition would have swiftly won them over as it always seemed to do.

Even for Jakob and his siblings, homecoming might have been overshadowed by some sense of estrangement. Home no longer offered the place of safety and security for all of them. Many young Mennonites were attracted by the chance to study in the larger cities of Russia or even abroad. Although some were happy to return to the home villages to serve their communities as doctors or teachers, others were being drawn in another direction. The opportunity to study away from the home setting was becoming a more significant influence on their lives. This could test how firm their ties were to the backbone values and faith of their home community.

Sonja and Katja came under the influence of Lenin's wife, Krupskaya, during the early days of Bolshevism in Petrograd and Moscow. Although women's education was supported to a degree with *Mädchenschulen* (Girls' high schools) in several of the larger villages, Krupskaya's campaign to educate the peasant masses and attack illiteracy would have impressed Sonja and Katja. And certainly her early brand of feminism might have appealed to these ambitious young women. But their dreams were ultimately of no avail and eventually they would both fall victim to Stalin's purges, spending time in forced labor camps.

How was Mary affected by this first meeting with the daily life of the people called Mennonites? On the long train journey of several days she might have speculated about the reception she would receive from Jakob's parents. The couple would probably have secured seating in first or second class comfort, which was still available on the trains; though it would later give way to crowded and uncomfortable open seating, denoting the social equality of communism. She might have stood in the corridor watching the countryside of Russia and then Ukraine slide slowly past the train window, wondering how outsiders were regarded by the village people. And in case she visualized herself coming into the church on her new husband's arm, did Jakob warn her that unlike the churches of the cities they may have attended, Mennonites separated men from women in their simple plain churches?

*Sonja Reimer as teacher in Moscow, 1920*

She might also have reflected that she was taking Jakob's whole faith and family on trust. But then, they also would face a young woman of a rather different background. Her musical ear was no doubt impressed with their beautiful singing in four-part harmony; and perhaps she was touched by their simple piety with its sense of God's closeness. Obviously, something was drawing her to this people and, though this first encounter with them was brief, it would take hold of her for many years to come. In the photograph she seems already part of the scene, blissfully unaware of how soon the peace of that way of life would be torn apart.

For the time being, however, she could enjoy the flourishing agricultural scene in the villages with the lush growth of the farmlands and local gardens. There were picnics and outdoor dinners under the beautiful acacia or mulberry trees. The warm climate only enhanced the heady scents of flowers and blossoms, creating a sense of idyllic beauty. Jakob's mother had a large flower garden, which Mary, with her green thumb, would have appreciated.

Although the ravages of war, so soon to overtake that tranquil life, were not being felt in their day-to-day life, some ominous signs were appearing on the social scene. Some of the larger estates were already being confiscated and the effects of the Land Liquidation Law of 1915 were threatening some landowners. Obviously also, the conscription of all young men under forty, like Jakob, was to soon have a devastating effect on the economy.

Jakob accompanied his young wife back to Petrograd in September 1915; and in October he joined a Red Cross ambulance train under the detachment of Purishkevich, a well-known Monarchist. While Mennonites were no longer exempt from military conscription, they had worked out an arrangement with the Russian government such that they could serve their country in various alternative services either in forestry or as Red Cross medical servicemen.[6] Mary resumed her job in Petrograd, where she could be visited by her husband whenever his leaves permitted.

Yet the young bride was not completely alone in the city. She would now be more drawn to associate with the community of young Mennonites clustered both in Moscow and also in Petrograd, pursuing their education or other work-related possibilities. They gathered together in much the same way that, in succeeding generations, young rural Mennonites have done in the cities of the West. For some, their need for vital fellowship drew them together. Others were just happy to associate with each other, and often found themselves enjoying some of the aspects of their youth, like food and music-making in a less restrictive environment and context.

---

[6] See Lawrence Klippenstein and Jacob Dick, *Mennonite Alternative Service in Russia: The Story of Abram Dück and His Colleagues, 1911–1917* (Kitchener: Pandora Press, 2002); and the diary of Jakob C. Reimer of Wiesenfeld [a different Jakob Reimer], *Experiences in a Medical Unit of the Imperialist Army* (Year 1, 1915–1916 and Year 2, 1916–1917) in the Reference Library of the Mennonite Historical Society of British Columbia, Abbotsford.

The circumstances of war put a different meaning on their togetherness; it was a togetherness that may have given Mary some sense of protection. Also, there were now those like Jakob, serving in the Red Cross medical corps, who would periodically be stationed in major cities. While in Moscow, many of them attended a large Lutheran Church in the city, possibly the one that was later claimed by the Baptists on Maly Vuzovsky Street. The young men enjoyed the fact that there was good German singing and reading, but found the liturgical services a little too formal. They welcomed more informal gatherings. Jakob's considerable musical gifts would have made him a welcome singer and accompanist at some of those occasions.

*Mennonite medical servicemen serving with the Red Cross in Moscow, 1915*

Later in Moscow during the 1920s, a small choir formed from these young folk and served in a smaller house fellowship that some of them frequented. The choir was directed by F.C. Thiessen, Harold's future father-in-law. A photograph of this group somehow found its way into the album that Erika had inherited from her Aunt Sonja. The choir includes her young friend, Katie Thiessen, who later married

Henry Klassen, CF's brother. Their friendship began during these years in Petrograd, continued in Moscow, and carried on for several years when Katie lived in Canada.

How did Jakob fare in the ambulance corps starting in 1915, those two years so early in the marriage, we wonder? Service in the Red Cross medical corps took Mennonite men into the very heart of the war effort in their homeland. It was an experience totally different from their life in the villages. They were assigned to the large trains which shuttled constantly back and forth from the battle zones to the stationing posts in various strategic cities like Moscow and Petrograd, Kursk and Orel, where the wounded received further treatment.

*Personnel, including Mennonite medical servicemen, on a Red Cross ambulance train*

The medical trains became a kind of primitive emergency unit, and each man would remain with a unit in that train for his entire time of service. The men would become a close team of brothers. Any that had not traveled far from their home villages would now get used to traveling by train, week after week, across the vast expanse of Russia. The huge lumbering hospital trains hauled the wounded and dying to cities that the medical servicemen only knew by name, where they endured extremes of weather and physical hardships hitherto unfamiliar to them.

The conscripts were subjected to a strict regime and discipline, overseen by Russian medical personnel, who were quite often women—something that was hard to swallow for some of the young Mennonite men. Some of the young "Madame Doctors" ruled over the young groups of Mennonite men with an iron fist, making them scrub and re-scrub the crude plank floors and repeatedly disinfect the bedding and hospital garb. This would have been particularly demeaning for the young men, who often felt their clean habits to be superior to those of their Russian neighbors.

Those unused to caring for the sick would have found their service experience particularly gruesome. There were few medical resources available, and many of the men wounded in battle received operations with limited help from anesthetics. But the young Mennonites drew on the deep caring heritage of their people, which held compassion as a major value. They were also grateful to be of service to their Russian homeland and to be drawn into the mainstream of its struggle at such a time.

By December 1915, the detachment that Jakob had joined was sent to the front in one of these ambulance trains. His detachment was part of the Purishkevich Monarchical Army that was loyal to the Tsar and his regime. Did Jakob have distinct Royalist leanings, we wonder? C.F. Klassen had two brothers who later enlisted with the anti-communist White Army that fought the Bolsheviks in the Russian Civil War (1917–1923). One was killed in action.

The Russian mail system served those working on these trains very well, so that Mary—all her life a faithful letter writer—would no doubt have corresponded regularly with her husband during this period. Perhaps from this period came the little photograph we had seen in Erika's album, the one taken by Mary of the desk displaying the portrait of herself with Jakob. The men would have shared with each other any food parcels they received by mail from their home villages. As food shortages became more critical, they also took advantage of their ability to pick up food items from the other villages along the train route, food items that were no longer available to their own families in the villages and even scarcer in Moscow.

As has been mentioned, Mary had been transferred to Petrograd, to a branch of the shipping company she had worked for in Riga. This would have meant that when Jakob's train took him to that city, they would have had a brief reunion since short leaves were allowed. But this was hardly the desired life of a young newlywed couple. This continued until June 1916, when Jakob was reassigned to duty as a driving instructor for the Red Cross in Petrograd, allowing for more time with his young wife through to the critical period of 1917.

As World War I wore on, there were more radical changes going on in Russia. Strikes, demonstrations, social unrest, food shortages, riots, marked the beginning of 1917. The economic and social effects of the war effort were being felt as Bolshevism gained ground, threatening to destroy the old way of life. The cities became the battlegrounds with daily hand-to-hand conflict between the factions; violence became an everyday occurrence. The young student population was increasingly getting caught up in the momentum towards a new Russia. The old imperialist order of the Tsar, with its vast system of nobility, was weakening and the Bolsheviks were gaining influence.

Back in Crimea the situation was rapidly descending into chaos. Though the robber bands that terrorized Ukraine did not reach into this region, there were other lawless elements including some of the Black Sea sailors that roamed the area, stealing and pillaging. It was no safe place for quiet villagers.

The year 1917 was a landmark year in Russia. In March, Tsar Nicholas II abdicated the throne and a Provisional Government under Prince Georgy Lvov was established. Then in July, Lvov resigned and Alexander Kerensky became Prime Minister, forming a new government. The murder of Tsar Nicholas II and his entire family on July 16 by the Bolsheviks was deeply shocking to the Mennonites. They had a profound respect for the traditions of the regime and especially Tsarina Catherine the Great, who had invited them to Russia in the first place more than 150 years earlier. The Tsar's picture held pride of place in many institutions, and even on the walls of many Mennonite homes. Now it seemed all those symbols of law and order were disappearing as the Bolshevik majority pushed out Prime Minister Kerensky to form a communist government in Petrograd at the October Revolution (November 7, 1917).

The times were getting harder and food was scarce. The Bolshevik Revolution was not universally recognized outside Petrograd and the country descended into civil war between those loyal to the Tsarist ways (White Army) and the new Workers' or Peasants' Army (Red Army). It became clear that the last stages of World War I did not bring relief, but only more troubles for everyone. This was a time of great upheaval in the Mennonite colonies. Red Army units swarmed their villages. Then, at Easter, April 1918, the German troops marched in and occupied the region. They were welcomed by the Mennonites as liberators. But any temporary relief from conflict was swiftly lost as Red Army units again moved in. The whole area of quiet agricultural settlements became a war zone. Marauding bands further terrorized the peaceful life of the Mennonites. Now hunger and destruction threatened their very survival, and some Mennonite villages formed militia units for self-defense, a measure that proved controversial in some circles.

Many were fleeing to Crimea in search of some respite from the fray. Drastic changes affected everyone living in the cities. Survival was a daily challenge. Food shortages and social disruption faced them on all sides. Clashes and bloodshed made life in the city dangerous and more and more untenable.

Once again, the young couple's thoughts turned to the peaceful home they had left in the village of Karassan. In 1918, at the end of World War I, Jakob's work as a driving instructor for the Red Cross came to an end at his demobilization; he then worked for a short time with the railway. The young couple faced both unemployment and food shortages, so they decided to move again to Karassan in 1918 and were again taken in by Jakob's mother.

How different the train journey must have been from their first trip together. Old class distinctions were swept away now. Gone was the genteel first-class travel option under the new communist regime. Trains would have been terribly overcrowded with suffering humanity, with everyone thrown together in the open seating arrangement. They frequently did not have enough seating at all for the masses moving around the country. Crowded and dirty, the long train ride would have made the journey a nightmare. Some journeys took several days to complete.

When they finally made it to Karassan, it was far from the peaceful scene they had envisaged. Civil war was now raging in Crimea. The Reds and Whites fought back and forth across the region. The couple tried to help Jakob's mother and the family during this time of great upheaval and great deprivation. For a time, the Bolsheviks appeared to be gaining control, but the White Army retaliated, first under the leadership of Lieutenant General Anton Denikin and then Baron Piotr Wrangel. Jakob would be forcibly recruited into Wrangel's army, serving as a medical serviceman for three months. The back and forth conflict continued unabated.

Mary must have felt like a liability in her husband's home village at a time when any extra mouth to feed was a burden. Yet her typical resourcefulness apparently took over. She told us later that for a short time her expertise as an accountant enabled her to work for an agricultural business in the area. At least that would have enabled her to make some small contribution to the struggling life of Jakob's family while he was gone.

Eventually, the White Army was routed and the Bolsheviks took control of Crimea in 1919. The Bolshevik Red Army's victory was short-lived, however. After a few months, the White Army, still under Denikin's leadership, achieved domination in the region. It would take until 1922, but eventually Ukraine, including Crimea, would also give way to the Bolsheviks and become a Soviet Republic.

In 1919, Mary returned again to her own family in Riga, Latvia, which had just become an independent republic. Jakob, however, was unable to obtain a visa to go to Riga, so he ended up back in Moscow, where Mary would eventually rejoin him.

How were the Mennonite colonists responding to the vast changes that were descending on their quiet village existence? It was clear to them that their way of life was severely threatened by the new views and values of the Bolsheviks who were gradually gaining power or were already in full control in the Soviet Republics. Their efforts to defend themselves against the demands of the newly emerging government in the Russian Republic would eventually lead to the formation of the *Allrussischer Mennonitischer Landwirtschaftlicher Verein* (AMLV) or Agricultural Union in 1923.

The diplomatic and advocacy efforts like the AMLV would call for much tireless work from young Mennonite leaders like C.F. Klassen and Peter F. Froese. In 1917, both men had already been involved in advocating for 37 Mennonites held under suspicion in Moscow by the Kerensky government, something that was reported at the 1917 meeting of the *Allgemeiner Mennonitischer Kongress* (All-Mennonite Congress). Both men were then chosen at Ufa in 1920 to represent the Mennonites of East Russia and Siberia in Moscow, coordinating relief efforts and negotiating with the Kremlin. The Mennonites hoped that their already long-established pattern of agriculture and self-government could become a model for the emerging Soviet society. But the explicit ties to their faith and values were to prove an impossible linkage for the atheistic, materialistic mindset of the Bolsheviks.

This struggle formed the context of the life of Mary and Jakob during this period, who, it appears, had now relocated to Moscow in 1920. It also defined the life of the small band of young Mennonites who found themselves thrown together there, including C.F. Klassen and Peter Froese. They were at the hub of the work that absorbed them for several years, seeking to coordinate the affairs of their people in the complicated matters of relating to the volatile new Bolshevik government regarding alternative military service, economic and agricultural reforms for the villages, and eventually the controversial issue of emigration.

Jakob had already been part of this group by virtue of his own ambulance service and later as a driving instructor for the Red Cross, and so would have already known CF. It seems clear that Mary had become fully part of the little circle of Mennonites now living in Moscow. This circle was drawn from several different parts of the Mennonite family of settlements, including some from Jakob's home area in Crimea and others from places like Halbstadt in the Molochna settlement and from Davlekanovo in the Ufa settlement. Mary had the chance to become better acquainted with these people, many of whom were to become dear friends in her future life in Canada. But that same association with all these people would become, as we shall see, critical for the fate of Jakob.

It is hard to comprehend what life, if any, this couple had together over this entire period. Even the strongest relationship would suffer severely through such times of stress. Work was hard to get and food was scarce. But now a new situation developed which would impact the group of young Mennonites in Moscow.

## The Time of Famine

This new situation grew out of the time of great hardship for the villages back in Ukraine. Social disruption had been followed by a typhus epidemic that took many lives. Added to this and all the suffering of the civil war, the poor crop harvests and disruption of food distribution were creating a desperate scene. Now a worse scourge descended in the shape of famine.

A new Associated Relief Committee was formed by the Bolshevik government and CF and Froese were appointed members, giving them the needed legal base for their continued activity in Moscow. But inefficiency and internal strife resulted in the committee swiftly being disbanded and several people being thrown into the dreaded Lubyanka prison in August 1921, including Froese and CF, and CF's brother, Henry, and incidentally, also a daughter of Tolstoy, and Maxim Gorky! They were all eventually freed after several days of interrogation, but it gave CF a taste of an experience that many others were to face in a much more disastrous way.

The famine did get the world's attention. The USA began to mobilize famine relief under the leadership of Herbert Hoover, who later became the American President and for whom my husband was named! Hoover encouraged Americans to respond to the famine through the American Relief Agency (ARA). Some of the young Mennonites still in Moscow were able to help out with this agency, including C.F. Klassen's brother, Henry. Jakob also worked for this agency in Moscow from 1922 to 1923.

Mennonites in America, however, desired to respond more specifically to the needs of Mennonite villages in Ukraine, Volga Region, Orenburg, and other regions in the Russian Republic, so they established a new Mennonite relief agency called Mennonite Central Committee (MCC) in 1920. MCC sent Alvin J. Miller to Moscow in 1921 to set up the American Mennonite Relief (AMR) office, which was tasked with finding ways to bring relief to the Mennonite villages that had suffered so much during the civil war at the hands of the anarchists (Makhno) and various invading armies.

*CF at the Moscow Mennonite Centre offices*

In order to comply with the Russian bureaucratic system, the AMR had to set up its office in Moscow. Needing local Mennonite help for its operation, the AMR found in the young C.F. Klassen an indispensable co-worker. It was a natural fit as CF was already working in Moscow on behalf of his Mennonite people as their representative in negotiations with the new Bolshevik government of Lenin. Many young Mennonite men, now released from their service in the medical corps, also helped the relief agency with driving, delivery of aid, and practical help.

Mary also became an essential helper to this agency, becoming secretary to the main officer of the work, Alvin Miller, who had arrived in Moscow from America in 1921. A photograph from this time shows Mary seated at her desk during the period when several different agencies shared a common building. The name, American Mennonite Relief, can be seen written in Russian on the front of her desk. She was a great asset to Miller with her considerable linguistic skills and experience as stenographer and typist. This meant that she found herself part of the core group at the hub of this work at its office, which was eventually moved to the new Mennonite Centre.

*Mary at the American Mennonite Relief office*

The need for the aid provided by the AMR was clear. Peter Froese reported that even the diet of the Mennonite Centre workers was meager in those years. The main nutrition came from roasted bread rolls and millet meal that was provided by the home villages!

These years were a watershed time for the people of Russia, and also for the Mennonites. These were critical years of decision, when distinct lines of loyalty were being drawn that were to affect the future of countless lives that would follow. Already many of the colonists were being helped to seek a better life by immigrating to North America. The small band of young people who made up the circle with whom Jakob and Mary were involved struggled daily in their efforts to give leadership and counsel to their scattered brothers and sisters. Some were by now convinced that their only hope for a future lay beyond the shores of Russia.

Not all in the Moscow group shared this conviction. Some, perhaps including Jakob himself, hoped that the Bolsheviks would yet usher in a more stable new society. Whatever hopes and dreams the couple had, an event in the present became more pressing—Mary gave birth to a son, Harold, on October 5, 1923. She now had a more urgent reason for a place to call home for the years that lay ahead.

*Mary with Peter Froese at the American Mennonite Relief office*

After helping for some time with the relief effort and parcels for the hungry, Jakob again got work as an engineer working at establishing low-voltage energy. This would have been work directly mandated by the new Bolshevik government. Erika wondered if such a step would also have seemed expedient in order to put behind him the period he served in the now defeated monarchist White Army. Employment would at least mean that he received a food card, and given the desperate food shortages in the city, that would have seemed crucial to their survival as a little family unit. Mary's ongoing work for the Mennonite relief agency would have proved critical in helping to provide for daily needs.

In her memoir, Nadezhda Mandelstam, wife of Russian poet Osip Mandelstam, relates how incredibly difficult it was to keep any semblance of a normal life and family during those years. The struggle for survival was all that mattered. She writes: "The years of Revolution—from 1918 to 1922—were as overwhelming as a natural disaster . . . death might come at any moment . . . blood flowed in every street, outside every home. Bullet-ridden corpses lying in the roads and on the pavements were a familiar sight to us all."[7] These were scenes that Mennonite people were reluctant to report, yet they also lived through this period. And, as Nadezhda Mandelstam reflects, it was amazing that any relationship could survive such horror and total disruption. Many relationships did survive these experiences. But not all were so fortunate.

Mary and Jakob's attempts to return to their respective home roots during these years were an indication of their difficulties, but also their desire to grasp at some stability and permanence. Yet in the end, they were unable, it seems, to build enough stability in their own little family to withstand the colossal forces arrayed against them. Ironically, it was only at the end of this period that they finally had a child. Harold reports that his mother told him that she left her desk at the Mennonite Centre and went straight to the hospital where he was born! But it may have been too late for the new life they had birthed to hold them together. Forces beyond their control were soon to tear them apart, one more fateful time.

It was in 1924, when Harold was still barely a year old, that Jakob left for Tashkent, which was at that time the capital of Turkestan. Had he received direct orders from the Soviet party that he could not refuse? Tashkent was soon to become the capital of the newly formed Soviet Socialist Republic of Uzbekistan. The ancient capital was being hurriedly developed to conform to the industrial surge of the new

---

[7] Nadezhda Mandelstam, *Hope Abandoned: A Memoir* (London: Collins and Harvill, 1974), 515.

communism. New factories, roads, and railways were being built. Jakob worked as an engineer, his chosen profession before the war. Was Jakob's leaving simply a practical matter about which he had no choice? Did he perhaps think it would be only a short period of separation, similar to those they had experienced while he was in the Ambulance Unit? As we have reflected on this key moment in Jakob and Mary's marriage, we wish we had greater clarity about it, especially in answer to Erika's repeated question as to the reasons for Jakob and Mary's subsequent divorce.

We have no evidence for the unfair inference we made in *Ambassador to His People*—that Jakob had carelessly abandoned Mary. The charge that he was a poor provider seems particularly harsh given the context of the Revolution. Anyone would have grasped at the chance offered an engineer to serve in Tashkent at a time like that. His leaving may appear to us independently taken, yet no one's affairs at such a time were very independent. Lives were constantly disrupted; people were moved around the country like pawns, leaving relationships fractured by the dislocated society. Survival was the order of the day.

Erika's repeated question, "Why did your mother and my father divorce?" may never receive a definitive answer. All we know is that after the many years of on-and-off separations that Jakob and Mary had experienced, this one was to be the last, and would be permanent. Erika's mother, Vera Protopopova, was a stenographer working at the hydroelectric plant where Jakob was employed; they met and developed a relationship soon after he arrived in Tashkent.

That haunting song Mary always sang as she sat at her piano, about the lonely figure on the highway, runs through my mind as I reflect on these events. Did she have a memory of his final leaving— Jakob making his way through the deserted streets of Moscow early one morning, as he made his way to the railway station to catch the train that would take him out of her life forever? Or was she now that lonely figure facing an unknown path into an uncertain future?

It is possible that more than physical distance had developed between these two people. Was there a deeper difference between Jakob and Mary, regarding their views of what the future might hold? Even though she welcomed some of the principles of the Bolshevik Revolution in its desire to benefit the masses and release them from the bonds of servitude to the wealthy aristocracy, Mary was convinced that the movement contained within itself harsh seeds of a crueler portent. She somehow sensed the heartless brutality that might be ahead for those who did not conform, and she feared for the treatment of those with differing views.

Jakob, on the other hand, may have shared the optimism of friends like Peter Froese, who hoped that things just might eventually turn out for the good. We know that Jakob's main interests in life revolved around his music, and the Russian cultural opportunities that were offered through it. We know nothing of his faith at the time. According to Erika, he never communicated any of those spiritual values to her.

By now, Mary was almost obsessed, like a mother bear, with the future of her young son, protecting him against all odds and already speculating on what would be the best course of action to ensure his safe future. Circumstances did not seem to be providing them a united strategy for survival in Moscow, with Mary assured of work at the Mennonite relief agency, but with Jakob unable to provide for his small family there.

There are some who feel that C.F. Klassen may well have had a role in coming between Mary and Jakob as the relationship between CF and the young secretary grew—they both worked side by side at the Mennonite Centre. That deep friendships were nurtured in this setting is undeniable; with the world crashing around them and with life and survival so fragile, things were anything but simple. Just when such friendships might turn into deeper relationships or when others might grow distant is not easy to pinpoint.

In 2000, after Herb and I had been back in Canada for five years, Erika's persistent inquiries led to the discovery of her father's interrogation record with the KGB. In that record, which we shall examine in greater detail later, we finally hear Jakob's own voice through the propagandist noise. His words give us more understanding of the delicate matter of these relationships. It startled me to hear in Jakob's testimony at his 1937 interrogation, that CF, Mary's second husband, had actually been a trusted friend to Jakob. Just days before his execution, we hear Jakob say, "C.F. Klassen was a good friend and a frequent visitor in our home.... After he left for Canada, I continued to write to him.... My son, who is now fourteen, lives with them."

For me, Jakob's testimony that CF was a trusted friend, and that Jakob's son, Harold, was now part of CF's family and being provided for by CF, challenged the speculation raised in some quarters: namely, that CF had destroyed Jakob and Mary's marriage. And as I have reflected on the situation in Moscow at the Mennonite Centre, I have sometimes felt that Jakob may well have asked CF to take care of Mary while he was gone. At any rate, he knew he had trusted friends who would support her, especially now that she had a child to care for, too.

But for some, the questions persist. I have tried to find answers to these questions from family members and the wider Mennonite community. I have only been met with speculation and more questions, and no incontrovertible evidence. We need to acknowledge such differing views concerning the failure of Mary's marriage, but none of us can ultimately be sure we have seen the whole picture.

Erika's unanswered questions will likely always remain unanswered, leaving a gap that persists and resists simplistic resolution. Instead, such a gap cannot help but get woven into the fabric that becomes a life's story, adding depth and texture to the particular story.

Mary and Jakob were divorced in 1925. It presumably happened after it became clear that Jakob was destined to remain in Tashkent, or when he had established a relationship with Erika's mother, Vera Protopopova. In the new climate of social affairs under Bolshevism, divorce had become very easy. Under the tsars, before the Revolution, divorce was very rare, and was frowned on both by the Russian Orthodox Church and Protestant groups, like Baptists and Mennonites. But now it could be obtained by a simple request to the courts from either party. The equality of the sexes, under the new values of communism, did away with the old patriarchal ways and exploitation of women. Now everyone was equal and couples worked side by side for the new emerging society.

Mary's marriage to Jakob had lasted almost ten years. Comparing the photograph of Mary as a young woman from Erika's album with photographs of the Mary towards the end of the 1920s, it is clear that these difficult years had taken their toll on her and that she had matured through them. I am grateful that a recent discovery of some of Mary's letters from these years, which will be shared in our next chapter, reveals her resilient spirit. She remained undaunted. Her faith and optimism prevailed against the gloomy clouds that were gathering over the little band of Mennonites in Moscow.

# 6

# Mary and C.F. Klassen in Moscow

Following Jakob's departure in 1924, Mary threw herself even more into the work of the Mennonite relief agency in Moscow. Her relationship with the young CF developed. They, along with the team at the Mennonite Centre in Moscow, had been working tirelessly since 1921, negotiating policy with Soviet officials and organizing relief aid for those in the Mennonite villages.

The main work of this time was negotiating new structures to enable Mennonite villages to coexist in a post-Revolution reality, a task that CF shared with his close friend Peter Froese, as outlined in the previous chapter. They had been friends since their student days in St. Petersburg and both felt called to serve their people in this way. Earlier they had worked side by side negotiating with the Bolsheviks issues like alternative military service for Mennonite young men, but now a new challenge faced them, negotiating agricultural reconstruction in Mennonite villages within the new communist framework.

As described previously, some still hoped that communism would not preclude reestablishing a viable way of life for the agricultural communities of the Mennonite colonies. This hope became the focus of the work for Froese and CF. The answer, they felt, was a new organization that would unite all the villages, defining and protecting their way of life and their values in the changing political climate of communism. This was the thrust of the mandate given to CF and Froese in the formation of a Mennonite Agricultural Union, the AMLV, which met for its first congress in October 1923.

## The AMLV

As I revisited the research we did when we wrote *Ambassador to His People*, I have gained a deeper understanding of just how stressful this period was for CF. Now from the perspective of Mary, I see how much she had to take on in supporting CF through the huge challenges he faced with the AMLV. It is difficult to comprehend how men like Froese and CF struggled daily, hour after hour, in the offices of the Kremlin itself, negotiating with some of the leading figures of the Revolution, seeking to salvage and reconstruct the Mennonite colonies and their way of life.

For the leaders of the Mennonite people, the AMLV was more than a human organization. It was a vocational calling from God, an instrument by which to save their people's values and their very existence in Russia. The AMLV mandate was to dominate the final years that Mary and CF spent in Moscow. It deeply affected their decision to finally leave Russia and helped me understand why processing that decision was so difficult for them.

The application for approval of the AMLV from the Bolshevik government was long and complicated. It was a daunting task, but one to which CF was equal in faith, expertise, and energy. But one key element continued to surface. It was becoming clear that they would need to downplay the religious aspect of their lives in the Mennonite villages, in order to appeal to the atheistic government of Lenin. For Froese, "One principle only lay at the foundation of the Union. That was the revival of agriculture, and in no way would the AMLV be given any religious responsibilities. The only issue was Mennonite agriculture, of which the historic importance to Russia was universally acknowledged."[8] But even with such a narrow mandate for the AMLV, some wondered if this was a price they were willing to pay.

When Alvin Miller first arrived in Moscow several years earlier in 1921, he was clearly overwhelmed by the situation that he found. Unlike descriptions from Russians like Nadezhda Mandelstam, mentioned in the last chapter, Miller's description helps us visualize the scene graphically, through the eyes of an outsider. He writes: "Everywhere in the city were the evidences of revolutionary upheaval—streets in bad condition, sidewalks worn out, rubbish and refuse strewn about, buildings generally dilapidated, houses in heaps of ruins . . . people shabbily dressed and emaciated wandered listlessly

---

[8] John B. Toews, ed., *The Mennonites in Russia From 1917 to 1930: Selected Documents* (Winnipeg: Christian Press, 1975), 202; see also John B. Toews and Paul Toews, eds., *Union of Citizens of Dutch Lineage in Ukraine (1922–1927): Mennonite and Soviet Documents* (Fresno: Center of Mennonite Brethren Studies, 2011), 219.

about on the streets. An atmosphere of suffering and hopelessness pervaded the city."[9]

Given CF's negotiating experience and extensive network, it was no wonder that Miller quickly recruited CF to help him as Russian representative in the famine relief to the starving villagers after the Revolution. This meant that CF and Mary crossed paths daily in the office of the Mennonite Centre that was relocated within the new building just acquired by the AMLV in 1923. It is no wonder that CF valued the prayerful care of the secretary at the Mennonite Centre, whom he met when he returned from those negotiation sessions every day. The extensive AMLV premises housed a number of relief groups, in addition to the Mennonite Centre, and residential accommodation for many of the workers on the second floor. Life in this building was a maelstrom of activity that defined Mary's final years in Russia.

Mary got to know Daria, the Russian wife of Peter Froese, a devout Baptist physician, who named her daughter, Cornelia, after Cornelius. After Jakob left for Tashkent, it seems feasible that Mary would have brought her young child to the Centre to be cared for daily by some of the young Mennonite girls that were helping other families with young children, like the Froeses and their friends, the Lehns.

The little community was a close-knit one, and is described by one of those young women, Anna Reimer Dyck, in her book *Anna: From the Caucasus to Canada*. The offices were all on the ground floor of the building. The second floor had eight rooms to house workers like the Froeses, CF, and Miller, as well as guests, including some of those who were processing their papers for emigration. Anna describes the many hours that were spent together around the samovar, discussing the direction of affairs in Russia and imagining the eventual outcome of the political scene there. Peter Froese identified with the working class. He had great hopes that the Revolution would give birth to a new and more just Russia, one where the values he espoused would prevail. CF shared his hopes to a degree, but increasingly had misgivings. And Mary, with an inner sense of urgency, felt that the best prospect for them all was to emigrate.

The AMLV was a highly organized network, encompassing the Mennonite settlements in the Russian Republic. It contained a detailed agricultural inventory of all the resources they had in the area of crop

---

[9] Peter C. Hiebert and Orie O. Miller, eds., *Feeding the Hungry: Russia Famine 1919–1925* (Scottdale: Mennonite Central Committee, 1929), 134; see also Herb Klassen and Maureen Klassen, *Ambassador to His People: C.F. Klassen and the Russian Mennonite Refugees* (Winnipeg: Kindred Productions, 1990), 50–51.

growth, seed production, animal husbandry, breeding, and so on. Froese and CF's role in the executive of this organization was very impressive. The energy they devoted to the work meant that their people could put forth a valiant attempt to convince the Bolshevik authorities that the life of the Mennonite settlements should be supported for the benefit of its people and of Russia. Froese, as chairman, and CF, as secretary, spent endless hours on all the bureaucratic paper work, and in meetings with officials in Moscow.

*AMLV staff, Peter Froese (middle, center) and CF (middle, far right), 1925*

In addition to his AMLV work, CF also helped the Mennonite relief agency (AMR) with trips to the famine-stricken Mennonite villages. As Alvin Miller's secretary, Mary would have observed how closely they depended on CF. She was part of documenting the reports that he filed of his visits to the needy Mennonite settlements. Such concerns would have appealed to her sense of compassion for the starving people, and no doubt gave her some satisfaction that she could be of some help herself with her own skills. It also gave her a glimpse into the heart of CF.

Later in Canada, both in Winnipeg and in British Columbia, Mary would often meet people who still remembered CF's visits to their villages in Ukraine or Siberia; they credited CF with rescuing them from starvation with the supplies he brought from America. She would smile at their characterization of him as a kind of folk hero!

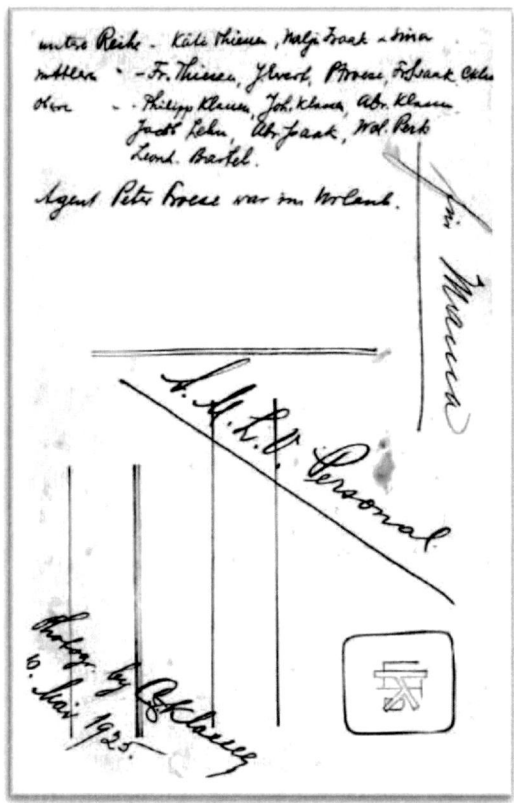

*Back of AMLV photograph identifying staff members, 1925*

Miller's glowing praise of CF is striking. At the first congress of the AMLV in Alexandertal (Old Samara), October 1923, which Miller attended as a guest, he referred to their work together in the famine relief as follows: "Klassen has not only been our right and left hand, but also our eyes, ears, and mouth. In our dealings with the authorities, Cornelius has been of invaluable help to me. . . . I have been able to delegate all the responsible matters to him. . . . No Russian Mennonite has given himself more totally to the cause of the relief work than he has."[10] In this effort, the cooperation of the American Mennonites with

---

[10] Toews, ed., *The Mennonites in Russia from 1917 to 1930*, 252; see also Klassen and Klassen, *Ambassador to His People*, 65.

their Russian brothers and sisters saved countless lives. Mary was getting a taste of the wider Mennonite communion that would claim her involvement for decades to come.

Life was not getting any easier in the city, as wave after wave of people passed through the Mennonite Centre, seeking help in their efforts to emigrate. Already in 1923 there had been 2,759 Mennonites that left Russia. The majority of these emigrants were from the Chortitza Mennonite settlement in Ukraine. They were sponsored by the *Verband der Bürger holländischer Herkunft* (Association of Citizens of Dutch Extraction) or VBHH based in Kharkov, the capital of Ukraine. This Agriculture Union was formed in 1922 under the direction of Benjamin B. Janz to advocate for the needs of Mennonites in Ukraine. In 1923, the AMLV Agriculture Union was formed to aid Mennonites from the rest of Russia in agricultural reconstruction, following the VBHH Ukrainian model.

Initially, families preparing to emigrate could apply as groups. The following year, the authorities demanded an application for each person, requiring even more paperwork from B.B. Janz in Khrakov and CF in Moscow. At the same time, David Toews in Canada was leading negotiations with the CPR, as the railroad had agreed to extend a Travel Credit to the emigrants. (That loan was to play a major role in CF's life in years to come in Canada as he traveled to collect its repayment.) In spite of the heavy workload, Janz, Froese, CF, and many others continued on undaunted. The number of emigrants increased each year, reaching a total of 5,940 in 1926, after which time it dramatically declined in each of the following years. The total number of Russian Mennonites leaving the Soviet Union for Canada between 1923 and 1936 was about 21,000.

Each case demanded hours of processing and negotiations with government offices. Through to 1928, the Agriculture Unions helped with these negotiations.

In the year 1924, CF's mother and siblings took the emigration step, giving up their life in Russia. Their general store in New Samara had been expropriated. Their father, Franz, had died. Two brothers had also died. One, by the name of Peter, had been drafted and served in the Russian White Army as a conscientious objector; he died in 1920. The other, Gerhard, was also conscripted and contracted tuberculosis. He died in a Moscow hospital, where CF was able to visit him until his death. CF and Mary later placed a wreath on his grave in a Moscow cemetery. CF's brother, Franz, and his wife, Katja Voth, with their little daughter, Elvira, and his brother, Jakob, were able to secure passage to Canada in October 1924.

CF's mother, Justina, and CF's seven remaining siblings came through Moscow and stayed at the Mennonite Centre while they prepared for the voyage to Canada set for October 1925. At that time, Mary and CF were not yet married and it is unclear to me whether Mary actually met her future in-laws. Since Mary worked daily at the Mennonite Centre where they stayed, it seems probable that she did meet them, though we do not know if CF would have revealed his growing relationship with her to them. We have been told that CF brought his sister, Elfrieda, for a visit to Moscow on an earlier occasion, where she did meet and take a liking to Mary. However it came about, as we shall soon see, Mary started writing very affectionate letters to the woman who became her mother-in-law, Justina Wiebe Klassen. Such intimacy is difficult to understand if they had never met. Mary must have made a good impression, in spite of whatever prejudices some may have harbored against her, as a woman of non-Mennonite origin and a single mother.

The Klassen family was glad to board the ship, having endured great hardship during the famine, often living only on beets for a lengthy period. They were grateful to see the end of their struggles and had great hope for a new life in Canada. CF would have liked to join them in their departure, but he was not yet ready to relinquish all his hard work and his hope for a turn-around in the affairs of the Mennonite people, given all he was doing with the AMLV. He did manage to accompany his family as far as Southampton in England and wish them Godspeed on their journey.

The second congress of the AMLV was held in Davlekanovo (Ufa) in 1924. But CF did not attend, citing a heavy workload that kept him in Moscow. However, he did send a stirring letter of encouragement to the gathered delegates. It reflects his continuing optimism, and his conviction that they should continue the struggle. After extending his heartfelt greetings, he writes: "I wish the assembly productive days. May the dim prospects, coupled with the ongoing drought in the various settlements, not take away courage from our representatives for the ongoing work of reconstruction. Our will to work and our faith in the victory must finally win out in the struggle with economic chaos. Our Mennonite agriculture in Russia will recover."[11]

---

[11] Toews, ed., *The Mennonites in Russia From 1917 to 1930*, 257.

These were brave words. But sadly they were not to be fulfilled.

Meanwhile, CF's attention was being drawn in another direction. Jakob's departure in 1924 and divorce in 1925 left Mary in a vulnerable position. Understandably, the thought of taking care of Mary would appeal to CF's deep sense of protectiveness, and cause him to pay constant attention to this courageous single mother and her little son. At first, Mary was reluctant to consider a second marriage and she feared the potential damage to CF's reputation. As the attraction between them grew, there was cause for much soul-searching; CF realized he was contemplating a relationship with a woman who, in the eyes of his church, would be viewed as an outcast.

When they both became convinced of what they must do, they realized that few church leaders would perform the necessary marriage ceremony for them. CF even took the step of resigning his formal membership in the Mennonite Brethren Church of Donskoi, New Samara, thus saving the church the pain of taking an action against him at a time when many people needed his help.

Minister Hermann Riesen from Old Samara, who was a trusted colleague of CF's on the AMLV board, happened to be in Moscow at the critical time and agreed to preach the wedding sermon from Genesis 35:3. The text's encouragement to trust in the Lord "who answered me in the day of my distress" must have reassured the couple and confirmed their decision, in spite of the opposition that may have been directed at them. Minister Johannes Klassen, also from Old Samara, conducted the ceremony and preached from Lamentations 3:19–24. "The steadfast love of the Lord never ceases, His mercies never come to an end; they are new every morning; great is Your faithfulness." The couple was indeed fixing their eyes on the mercy and compassion of a God who was well acquainted with the extraordinary circumstance that they were facing. It was September 11, 1926.

A visitor passing through Moscow and staying at the Mennonite Centre at the time of the wedding ceremony was John B. Toews. JB, as he came to be known, was a nineteen-year-old student from Alexandertal at the time, emigrating from Russia with his sister. He was to become a lifelong friend of the couple in Canada, where he became president of the Mennonite Brethren Bible College in Winnipeg, and then seminary, church, and mission leader in the USA.

A new chapter now began for the little family. CF, Mary, and young Harold moved together into one room of the Mennonite Centre. (Years later my husband and I with our firstborn, Tanya, also lived in one room at the London Mennonite Centre!) I had always imagined

Mary working side by side with her husband at the Mennonite Centre, serving the needs of his people in the settlements and the growing group of Mennonites preparing to leave Russia. But as a rather typical Mennonite father, it seems that CF felt it was his duty to find a girl to help Mary in her many tasks, as she expanded her responsibilities to include the role of mother. And a year later, when CF and Mary had their first son together, Walfried, CF hired a second girl to help Mary.

*CF, Harold, and Mary in Moscow, 1927*

That might seem surprising, since these must have been difficult times financially. But they clearly tried to preserve as many aspects of the old life as possible. Taking *Kindermädchen* or young girls into the family to help with the children was an old Mennonite custom, as much for the benefit of the young girl as for the help it gave to the young mother. These girls were not "maids" in the sense I would recall from an English culture.

I have since learned from my nephew, Neil, Walfried's son, that one of the nannies who cared for Walfried in Moscow was named Nina Shokovskaya. Apparently, her father, Count Shokovskoi, sometimes brought his daughter to the village of Abramtsevo, where she played with some children from Mennonite families living nearby. When the circumstances of the Revolution overtook them, the Count and his wife fled to England, leaving their daughter behind with her Mennonite friends to rejoin them as soon as she could. Arriving in Moscow, Nina was put in contact with CF, who hired her as a nanny. Sadly, she never succeeded in joining her family in England.

*CF and Mary with nanny, Nina Shokovskaya (left), 1927*

An additional little genteel touch that harkens back to their first years of marriage is now in the possession of my nephew, Randy. It is a beautiful wooden carved desk set and pen holder, possibly from Mary's past in Riga. On the back is inscribed, "For Christmas 1926, from Mary."

Mary always had a hankering for the country during the summer months and a longing for the peaceful life away from the problems and burdens of their work in the city. Somehow, in the midst of these difficult times, the young couple did manage a brief break. A happy photograph from this period shows them enjoying such a time; on the back of the photograph in CF's writing: "At the dacha in Tarasovka, 23 verst [about 23 km] from Moscow on the Northern rail line." In Mary's arms is her new young son, Walfried. CF is also gazing fondly at his firstborn. Nearly four years old now, Harold is leaning on his mother's shoulder, looking somewhat pensive. The date on the back is September 1927.

*CF and Mary with Harold and baby Walfried, 1927*

CF continued his tireless work for the Mennonite people, though a future for them in Russia seemed more and more impossible. Nevertheless, he continued to speak faith and optimism to the gatherings of the AMLV. But the negotiations with the Bolshevik government were becoming more and more difficult. Ultimately, it was the faith connection underlying the life of the colonies that became the issue. Although the Mennonites had agreed to downplay that dimension, hoping they could save their existence alongside atheistic communism, it became the breaking point. It was a devastating moment for them all when, in late spring 1928, the Bolsheviks finally stepped in and dissolved the AMLV. They said the Union could never be allowed to exist because of its Christian faith convictions and its separatist Mennonite way of life.

An unnamed communist economist, quoted later by CF in a letter, summed it up this way: "The AMLV . . . nourished the illusion among the Mennonites that the Mennonites had a right to their own cooperative and to individual development. . . . It had always been a handicap in the program of Sovietizing the Mennonite colonies. . . . It had been a mistake in every respect for the central government to authorize the establishment of the AMLV, thereby promoting a Mennonite separatism which was intolerable in view of the Bolshevik policy toward nationalities in Russia."[12]

The dissolution was a crushing blow to CF and Froese. They felt that years of sacrificial work on the part of hundreds of people was destroyed. And it was the end of CF's hope that a viable life for the colonies could be reestablished. But it was particularly bitter for him to consider emigration, knowing that not all of the Mennonite people would be able to leave with him. He had been acting as a kind of captain for his people. How could he leave the sinking ship? There would be some who remained and would have to face the bitter consequences.

## Emigration Prospects

The leaving-staying crisis was a hard one for the newly married couple to live through together. How did Mary, a young mother with two children, help her husband through this time of watching his life work crumble? I have often wondered how she dealt with all that. Was it a heavy burden for her, or did her usual optimism somehow prevail? It is good that my speculation on this subject was recently dramatically stopped in its tracks by the discovery of some letters from Mary to her

---

[12] Cornelius F. Klassen, "The Mennonites of Russia, 1917–1928" *Mennonite Quarterly Review* 6/2 (April 1932): 77; see also Klassen and Klassen, *Ambassador to His People*, 77.

mother-in-law in Canada, in the closing months of 1928, during those difficult days in Moscow.

I was startled to read their tone and to sense the resilient spirit of this young woman at such a crucial time in her life. It should be remembered that she may only have met her future mother-in-law once as the family was leaving Russia. Yet the evident affectionate bond shows a side of Mary that we, her children, all came to love and appreciate—her swift acceptance and warm relational way with people.

In Mary's letter it is touching to see how she recounts the constant humor and teasing that went on between her and Cornelius, as if it somehow carried them through the underlying tensions of their life. It reminds me of something I always noticed in Mary—her playful way of cutting through any over-seriousness or pomposity to the real person confronting her.

There are three letters typed in German on the fine onion skin paper of Soviet office supplies, now yellowed with age. I remind myself that these letters are over 80 years old! The first is dated May 1, 1928, just after the devastating news of the decision dissolving the AMLV.[13]

*Dear Mama, sadly much time has passed since I last wrote to you, though I had firmly promised to write regularly. But it hasn't happened! Dear Mama, you write in your last letter that you, too, were always very busy all your life. I imagine you were much busier than I am. I actually have a lot of help with two children and two maids! I could be enjoying a leisurely life and, if it is not so, it's my own fault! I'm a bit of a "Mennische Tante," always of the opinion that nothing happens without me. I often tell Cornelius that the comforts of life I now enjoy won't last forever, yet I run myself ragged and think I must oversee everything. In Canada I probably won't have two maids when the children are older, but Cornelius laughs and says that then there may be others, a boy or a girl, God willing! Well that's just small talk, but I don't worry about such things. I don't indulge in worrisome thoughts at all, though our future does look very dark.*

Amidst all the friendly, self-deprecatory small talk, this is the first hint of the circumstances they are actually facing. The letter continues in a similar tone.

*The summer is before us, but we can't rent a dacha without income. I still keep hoping that when everything closes down here, we may still get our passports and get away. Cornelius laughs at me and says we don't have the money to do that. I wonder if we could at least get cheaper passports and go as far as Riga, if we can't afford to go further. But what would we live on there? The people there are all very*

---

[13] Mary's letter to Justina, dated May 1, 1928, with English translation, is part of the Mary Brieger Klassen personal papers collection, Centre for Mennonite Brethren Studies, Winnipeg.

*poor. I come up with all kinds of ideas. Sometimes I pester Cornelius to tell me what he's thinking—how everything will work out, but he prefers not to speak of such things when we don't have the slightest inkling about them. Who can see into the future?*

*Today is May 1st and people are all out on the streets.*

Evidently, May 1st is a day of celebration, Labor Day or International Workers' Day. Mary goes on to tell her mother-in-law about the renovations to their rooms in the Mennonite Centre, the wallpapering and the dining room conversion, which Mary says she has already explained to her. Then she continues, alluding to the demise of the AMLV.

*Yesterday the office was cleared out. They all found it very difficult. It is very sad to see a cause die. So much work and energy has gone into it, all for naught. How sad. It may take months before everything is resolved, and then I hope we're on our way! Ach, Cornelius will laugh at me!*

Here she reveals the underlying tension they are facing as a couple. Her genuine sadness for CF, however, is the opening of the door she has long waited for! She then launches into more banter and small talk.

*Dear Mama, I was happy that you forbade Cornelius to spank little Walfried. Naturally he laughed at me, as he has often advised me to spank him when he's naughty, but has never done so himself. I will tell him he is not allowed to spank him before autumn until Walfried is well over a year old. But he is a naughty little boy. I can do nothing with him. I will have to be patient with him a little longer!*

Then there is more about their runny noses, their recovery, her wish for a garden, the weather, a visit to the grave of Gerhard, and how happy she is for the sunshine on this May Day—all matters of interest to the heart of a grandmother far away. She concludes:

*We send our very best greetings to you all, and especially to you, dear Mama. Heartfelt kisses from your Mary.*

Along the side CF has added a handwritten note to his brother, Franz, working in Steinbach, Manitoba, and a note to his brother, Henry, and his wife, Katie, signing off with:

*Heartfelt greetings to you all, Cornelius.*

He does not add anything of his own heartbreak here at the closing of his life's work in Russia; but he surely must have communicated that to his brothers elsewhere. Exactly what Mary means by the clearing out of the office is not spelled out. But according to usual Soviet protocol, it was a harsh process of destruction and confiscation of records, as well as reclamation of offices for government use. Miraculously, years later, the meeting minutes of

AMLV came to light, enabling some of what has been shared here to be known.

The next letter is from June 10, 1928.[14] Mary opens with apologies for the time that has elapsed since her May Day letter. Then she continues:

*I always look forward to your letters and recently you have strongly invited us to come to Canada. I would love to come right away, but Cornelius is quite sure there will be no passports for us, but perhaps we should try anyway. I would like to leave here right away and spend the summer at the sea somewhere and come to you in the autumn. If Jascha is ready to settle in Winnipeg, then you would have all your children around you. Wouldn't that be a lovely life? We will see what is in store for us. We do have a Counselor who will show us the way, if we pay attention to His voice.*

*Dear Mama, I must tell you what I just told Cornelius. I have started the liquidation process! I just sold one of my summer hats! I've laid aside the money to pay for our travel expenses. . . . Franz sent something in his last letter and I have added to that as well, so you see dear Mama, even if it is a modest sum and not to be taken too seriously, it is a beginning.*

Mary always had a reputation for stylish hats! Hopefully her mother-in-law saw the humor of this joke, particularly in their penniless situation. Accounts of domestic life continue with reports of vaccination for the boys and their reactions, more renovations to their rooms, including a bathroom, one that will be used by all the residents and might be appreciated more by those that are to follow. Also, that their two helper girls, Nina and Katja, are sleeping in their kitchen, and that her two boys are the noisiest in the place!

*Today we received a letter from my sister in Riga. She urges us again to come to Riga. They would love it if we would stay there forever. But they are all very poor and it is difficult to make a living. It would be better for us to come to Canada and have them follow us later, when we are more settled and more able to make a living. At present though, our prospects are very dark. How could we make a living there?* Kommt Zeit Kommt Rat [*with time comes wisdom*]. *Our heavenly Father will provide, about that I don't worry. We want to put it all in His hands. However He leads will be good. Our work here will soon be done. Cornelius has work for one more month.*

*Dear Mama, we are so thankful that you write so often and that you are all praying for us. In return, we all pray for you and all the family. He will do all*

---

[14] Mary's letter to Justina, dated June 10, 1928, with English translation, is part of the Mary Brieger Klassen personal papers collection, Centre for Mennonite Brethren Studies, Winnipeg.

*things well and will cause everything to come out as it should. With hugs and kisses hoping that we shall all meet you soon in person, your Mary.*

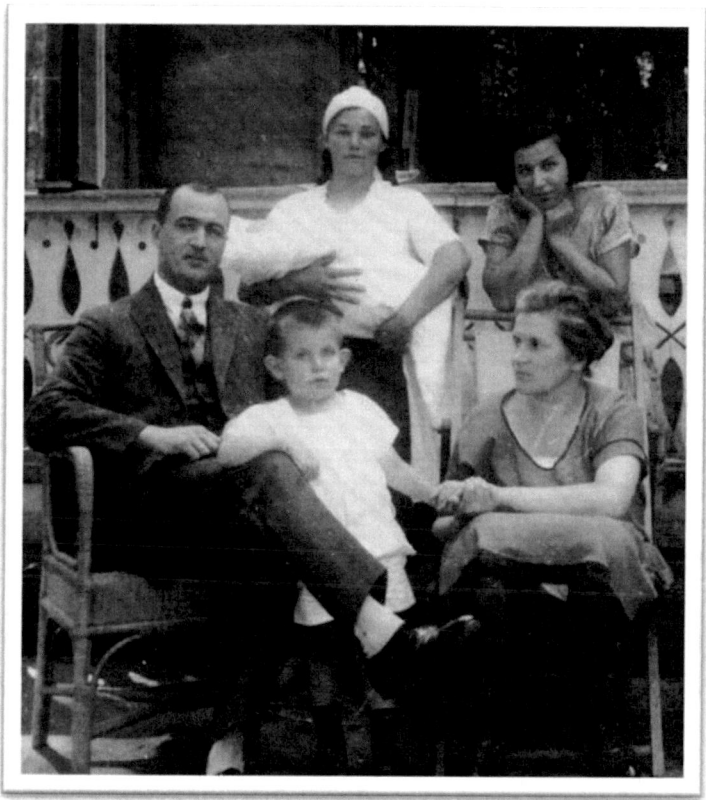

*CF, Harold, Mary, with nannies, Katja Voth and
Maria Epp (standing in back, Maria holding Walfried), 1927*

The third letter is dated June 26, 1928, the day before Walfried's first birthday.[15] Mary writes a lot about the two little boys' life and antics as they wrestle one another in the little playpen, which she surveys as she writes. She wishes that her mother-in-law could be with them to celebrate the birthday. After commenting on the weather, she writes:

---

[15] Mary's letter to Justina, dated June 26, 1928, with English translation, is part of the Mary Brieger Klassen personal papers collection, Centre for Mennonite Brethren Studies, Winnipeg.

*And that is how everything is here right now, dear Mama, everything is undecided. Cornelius' work will soon end, but he is immediately offered other work. If something will come of it we don't know. Or whether he should pursue it, we don't know either. Cornelius has no clarity about what he should do. And I am always encouraging him to apply for passports, and then we will see if we can leave. If we get them, we leave; if we don't, we stay. Lehns will get their answer the day after tomorrow. It seems to me that Cornelius is waiting for their result. If they get them, we apply, too. But I don't think we should wait for anything, but just apply. . . . If we don't get them, we will just have to adjust to that and see how we can make a living here.*

*Hermann Riesen was here for two weeks and talked a lot with Cornelius about the Amur region. I do not have any desire to go there. If we get away from here at all, we should go to Canada. We'll never get passports, if we don't apply; but it seems to me, dear Mama, that Cornelius is having a hard time with this decision. He doesn't know what he should do.*

Mary has finally put her finger on the problem that keeps resurfacing—the inner struggle that her husband is going through. Was it a fear that all his political involvement would exclude him from obtaining permission to leave? Was it a persistent guilt over abandoning his fellow Russian Mennonites that still needed him? Or perhaps he regretted that now, bound up with his own dubious fortunes, was the destiny of his wife and children? And what were the job offers? Amur, a region in Siberia, might offer some opportunity for renewing the network of Mennonite settlements. But that might offer the prospect of a difficult life ahead for his family. (And had CF taken the assignment, my husband, Herb, son number three, would have been born in Siberia and not Winnipeg!)

Whatever the reason for his endless ambivalence, Mary was clear: they should apply and take their chances to set in motion the emigration process that she was so eager to begin. Her faith and optimism all told her that this was the only alternative. She concludes her letter:

*Please Mama, don't stop inviting us to come. We do really want to come, but it all seems so impossible! You know how much Cornelius wants to see you, but he always thinks he's needed here. He'll laugh at me again and say, you keep repeating yourself over and over! You don't know what you're talking about. It's true! He wants me to get a little job and start putting money aside for our travel. I already told you about selling my hat. I would gladly begin tomorrow liquidating everything and then we could leave. Yes, here I go again, repeating myself again!*

*Walfried and Harold send you a goodnight kiss, dear grandma!*

So the situation continued with Mary constantly urging her husband to apply for their emigration papers. For her it was urgent. Life was becoming more and more difficult. CF was daily preoccupied with the needs of those who were coming to Moscow with a sense of urgency to get out while they still could. Finally, however, CF did complete the paperwork for their emigration passes, not holding out much hope that they would be granted. Since he was so absorbed with helping others, the task of submitting the paperwork and caring for the needs of the family fell to Mary herself. She recounts that she went daily to the appropriate authorities, applying and pleading for the correct papers. Why were the authorities making it so difficult? Was it CF's reputation? Did the fact of her divorce, or the need to have Harold's name changed to Klassen complicate matters?

Mary made repeated trips to the offices. There were times when they felt the gates would close before they got permission to leave. One can imagine her determination as she returned day after day with her petition, and her discouragement at the bureaucracy for their intransigence. People were prepared to pay any price to secure their passage out of Russia. Though the new political reality despised the days of corruption under the tsars, bribery was endemic to the Russian way of doing business. We have no knowledge of what it cost Mary to obtain their visas, but she would gladly have parted with any treasured family heirloom for the life of freedom that she valued higher than anything else. But whatever it cost, it was a day of great jubilation when she returned to the apartment one evening and triumphantly placed beside CF's plate at the supper table the required papers that would be their ticket to freedom in the West! CF, too, was surprised and was finally prepared to take it as a sign from the Lord that they should leave.

Now it remained to make the plans for the great trip out of Russia, following in the footsteps of the thousands who owed their new life in the West to the untiring work of CF and other leaders during those critical years in Moscow. On September 24, 1928, CF and Mary with their two sons boarded a train for Riga, as countless Mennonites had before them. Passing through the famous Red Gate—the point where so many Mennonite émigrés burst into songs of praise for their deliverance—they left Russia filled with mixed emotions.

They stopped in Riga for one final visit with Mary's sisters. Leaving their two little boys with them, CF and Mary made a swift visit to some of their friends in Germany, including Benjamin H. Unruh at Thomashof near Karlsruhe. Collecting their children back in Riga, they crossed the channel to England. On November 30, 1928, they left

Liverpool on the CPR steam ship, *Duchess of Atholl*, arriving in St. John, New Brunswick, on December 8, 1928.[16]

One can only imagine the varied emotions that occupied the little family on that week-long ocean voyage to a new homeland. They had been in constant communication with CF's mother and siblings in Winnipeg, so had some idea what was in store for them there. Mary, now pregnant with her third child (Herb), might have had understandable anxiety about relating to her new in-laws, especially given the circumstances of the marriage. While she appears to have been on good terms with her mother-in-law, perhaps she wondered about one or two of the siblings whom she had known while she was Jakob's wife. Would they really now accept her as their brother's wife? What kind of welcome would they give her now? And how would she fit into the closely knit Klassen family in Winnipeg?

She and CF left behind them in Russia a nation swiftly spiraling downward into the brutal 1930s under the leadership of Joseph Stalin. With the New Economic Policy failing, the Soviet society was floundering. Germans were increasingly subject to paranoid surveillance and arrests. Life in the Mennonite villages was quickly disintegrating. Confiscation of property and forced collectivization of Mennonite factories, estates, and farms ruined the way of life that had taken over a hundred years to construct. Families were torn apart.

CF's colleague and good friend, Peter Froese, was arrested soon after CF and Mary emigrated. Froese spent almost ten years in various prisons, first the Lubyanka, then Butyrka (both in Moscow), then in Yaroslavl, and finally in Orel. In June 1939, he was transferred via Krasnoyarsk to Mariinsk in the Kemerovo District, where he worked briefly as a farm laborer and in house construction for 5 months until January 1940. He was hospitalized in Mariinsk and released on October 15, 1940, exactly eleven years after his arrest. Froese was one of the few who managed to return.

The famous Russian painting by Ilya Repin (1844–1930), called the *Unexpected Visitor*, depicts a scene in which a political exile unexpectedly comes back home; bedraggled and unrecognizable, he stands in a room faced by a fearful and incredulous family. Such scenes would occur for Mennonites in the decades to come.

CF and Mary, on their way to Canada, were spared such experiences, but they carried with them the pain and suffering of their Russian Mennonite brothers and sisters who remained.

---

[16] Canadian Mennonite Board of Colonization card number 4972.

# 7

# Those That Remained

The picture that came to me often while writing this book was one of a tapestry. I saw the tapestry of Mennonite life in Russia, green and peaceful, suddenly torn to shreds by the Revolution, and its people scattered far and wide.

## A Mennonite Tapestry

*All down the years their lives were bound together;*
*A Tapestry of colors, joys, and tears;*
*Shared journeys, vistas, harvestings, and feastings;*
*The sounds of laughter and the songs of praise.*
*Till strife and conflict break upon the Quiet,*
*Discord, despair, disturb the peaceful scene.*
*The Tapestry is torn, life rent asunder,*
*And lofty hopes lie dashed upon the green.*
*Lives that were once entwined face separation,*
*Homes are forsaken, loved ones left behind.*
*The fabric of belonging is unraveled,*
*And we are left with fragments in our hands;*
*The severed threads of leaving and remaining,*
*That only Time, and God Himself can mend.*

When CF and Mary fled Moscow in 1928, not only was his life's work in ruins, the very fabric of Russian Mennonite way of life was in shreds. Behind every Mennonite who succeeded in escaping from the Soviet Union, there stretched a long dark shadow. This shadow spread to engulf a huge community of less fortunate people who, usually through no fault of their own, were destined to stay on in that land of sorrow. Many of them faced immeasurable suffering and cruel death.

This shadowed community can collectively be called, "those that remained." The stories of these people are less familiar. But with fresh opportunities for immigration to West Germany in the 1970s and 1980s, and with the recent disintegration of the Soviet Union in the 1990s, more of those stories are coming to light.

That day in 1993 at our Moscow apartment, when we were confronted with a hitherto unknown chapter of our own family's story, was a critical moment for our understanding of the whole Mennonite story of this generation. For me, Jakob represented that shadowy group of those that remained, those who had been forgotten or blotted out of the consciousness of the nation calling itself the Soviet Union, and even of some who called themselves Mennonites. But this group was not totally forgotten, for they were carried in the hearts and prayers of many who came to our part of Canada and who daily agonized about the fate of those they had not heard from for decades.

In our own family, we had never heard Jakob's name, or known that he had once been a valued part of our mother's life, much less the forebear of many of our extended family in Canada. We had not known of his existence or anything about his life, after his ways parted from Mary's. Now it seemed that he was just one of that innumerable remnant of those who remained. It subsequently seemed that during the balance of our time in Russia, we were to be introduced to many representatives of that unhappy cast. And as we met them, they seemed to be linked to us through Jakob as our own kith and kin.

It was of course understandable that our ignorance of Jakob was due to a choice Mary had made. It also meant that very late in his life, Harold had been given information about his own father, information that sadly he had never learned from his mother during her lifetime. Why did she feel unable to share more of this information with him, we wondered? Was it her maternal instinct to protect him from pain? Or was she afraid of the Mennonite rumor mill that she so studiously avoided during her life?

It must also be recognized that her knowledge of Jakob's ultimate fate was actually hidden from her over the years. What sadness she would have endured to know the high price he had paid for his choices. It would have been painful to have burdened Harold with any speculation about those possibilities. And then, too, she must have appreciated how thoroughly CF embraced Harold as his son. For whatever reason, there was only silence.

When Harold made the trip of a lifetime with his wife, Ruthie, to Moscow later in 1993, he returned to Canada with newfound knowledge about his father and spent the remainder of his years processing the implications for his own identity and that of his offspring. But there was further information about Jakob that would only come to light after Harold's death in 1996. With the disintegration of the Soviet Union in 1991, the time would come when the once-secret KGB files would become available to the public, files that would help us learn more about Jakob.

So here we pause in our journey of discovery to look at the place Jakob occupies in the suffering shared by his kin. Jakob was one of thousands whose full stories have rarely been told in the wider fellowship of the Mennonite people. These untold stories are the deeper colors of the tapestry of suffering, without which the full pattern of the years remains incomplete.

Already during our time in Moscow, we had been meeting people across the entire spectrum of Soviet society who had one thing in common: they had someone in their family circle who had suffered under Stalin's purges. There was hardly anyone we met who did not have a story about a relative who had been "repressed" or sent into exile or to the Gulag. Part of the pain these families endured was their lack of definite knowledge about the ultimate destiny of their loved ones. Many of them, like Erika, were hungry to discover more information about their loved ones and their fate. We met few, however, who were as persistently diligent about the search as she was.

The Mennonites who remained suffered the same fate as countless other Soviet citizens. For the thousands who had escaped from Russia in the 1920s, there were countless others who were turned back and scattered beyond the Urals to the frozen wastelands of Siberia and the far north. Others were sent across the eastern parts of the Soviet Union, even to the farthest flung Asiatic Soviet Republics. Deaths multiplied with every new phase of hardship and persecution. In the years 1936–1938 alone, the pinnacle of the suffering, close to 9,000 Mennonites (mostly men) were imprisoned, exiled, and executed.[17] Few

---

[17] Peter Letkemann, "Mennonite Victims of the 'Great Terror,' 1936–1938" *Journal of Mennonite Studies* 16 (1998): 37. Letkemann also notes that the 9,000 "taken" were about 8 to 9% of the Mennonite population in Russia at the time, which he estimates to have been about 100,000. He argues that the ratio is at least four times higher than that of those "taken" from the non-Mennonite population, largely because the Mennonites were prosperous, religious, anti-communist, and identified as German. Through to 1956, when the remaining internal exiles were finally released, it is estimated that a total of 30,000 Mennonites perished in the "Soviet Inferno." This number includes those who were arrested, imprisoned, and executed or exiled and then later perished in forced labor camps. See also Peter Letkemann, "The Fate of

stories filtered out to the praying relatives in the West, and many separated spouses finally gave up the long hope for reunion in this life.

A deep silence descended on the communication between the parts of the Mennonite family on both sides of the great divide, though miraculously some correspondence filtered out to the West, including one collection of letters recently published from the Gulag years.[18] In one instance, so the story goes, the trains hauling those arrested to their place of exile were pursued by bands of children, who would pick up the letters dropped onto the tracks by the desperate prisoners. By some miracle, these letters reached the West by mail. But for many, a curtain of silence descended on the formerly close family ties that had bound them tightly together. When we came to Moscow, little did we realize that we were to be granted a glimpse behind that curtain, stretching back to that moment in Mary and Jakob's life when their paths were forever separated—the moment that had made all the difference.

During our years in Moscow we met people who had survived these years. Even before we met Erika, we had been interested in meeting some of the remnant of Mennonites that had remained in the Soviet Union throughout the difficult Soviet years. Of course it was a bit of a stretch to call them Mennonites, since those who had not been killed had been banished to some of the far reaches of the Soviet Empire and forbidden to declare or practice their faith. The brutal system had worked all too well in many cases. But early in our time in Moscow, we began to meet people with Mennonite names who came to us inquiring about their history and indeed their identity. I began to refer to them as "trace" Mennonites, in that they, like trace minerals, held within themselves some traces of their earlier identity, albeit now irrevocably mixed with many other things.

## Moscow Mennonite Centre

Halfway through our time in Moscow, together with Lawrence and LaVerna Klippenstein, the interim country representatives for MCC, we opened the Moscow Mennonite Centre on November 15, 1992. It was to be a place where people could come and discover more about the

---

Mennonites in the Volga-Ural Region, 1929-1941" *Journal of Mennonite Studies* 23 (2008): 181–200; Marlene Epp, *Women Without Men: Mennonite Refugees of the Second World War* (Toronto: University of Toronto Press, 2000); and Anne Konrad, *Red Quarter Moon: A Search for Family in the Shadow of Stalin* (Toronto: University of Toronto Press, 2012).

[18] Ruth Derksen Siemens, *Remember Us: Letters from Stalin's Gulag (1930–1937)* (Kitchener: Pandora Press, 2008).

history of the Mennonites in the Soviet Union. This became the third Mennonite Centre described in this memoir! It was housed in the large three-room apartment near Moscow University that I described earlier in the first chapter. The front room overlooked the central leafy courtyard and housed our modest library. We held our Sunday afternoon meetings there. A second room served as the office. The third room contained the usual Soviet-style pullout sofa bed, where we slept; and it held our personal effects, a tiny desk, and our books. There was even a tiny balcony that looked out onto a quiet side street.

*Moscow Mennonite Centre library with MCC workers, 1993: back row, left to right, Lawrence Klippenstein and Herb Klassen; middle row, Ben and Erna Falk, LaVerna Klippensein; front row, Mary Raber and Maureen Klassen*

The Centre at first served as a place where visitors could connect with us, particularly Mennonite tourists and workers. The front room also had a sofa bed that doubled as a guest bed for visitors. Two such visitors included Myron Augsburger, former president of Eastern Mennonite University and theology professor, with whom I had studied while at Goshen Seminary, and John Bernbaum, who eventually founded the Russian American Christian University in Moscow. We also hosted tour groups from Tabor College and Lithuania Christian College, where our son, Steve, was teaching at the time. These groups would crowd into our front room with many questions about our life and work in Moscow.

Our Sunday afternoon meetings were a gathering of an assortment of interested people; they came to hear presentations on the Bible or the Mennonite story from speakers like Mary Raber, MCC country director, or Walter Sawatsky, MCC Soviet Union specialist. Gathered around the samovar over tea and cake, we enjoyed many discussions and good fellowship as well as times of singing and prayer. It reminded me of the days many years before at the London Mennonite Centre. But most of all, this was the place where many of these "trace" Mennonites would seek us out.

For example, there was the army major with the family name of Wallman, married to a Russian Orthodox "Old Believer." His father had owned a large factory in Ukraine, the Lepp-Wallman factory in the Chortitza colony. He knew very little about the Mennonites, but when he heard about us, he came asking whether we could baptize him! It became clear that there would need to be a great deal of further discussion on the matter, but he did spend considerable time reading the *Mennonite Encyclopedia* that was housed in our library in the front room, learning about his roots. It turned out he was a distant relative of our daughter-in-law's family in Canada, and later visited us there.

Then there was the very fine Russian Orthodox icon painter, Natasha Rempel, who came and shared the life story of her father, Peter P. Rempel, who had died in 1942 at one of Stalin's forced labor camps in Arkhangelsk, in the far north. Natasha's father had been a Mennonite pastor and she was convinced he was a saint. After telling his story to Father Alexander Men, he encouraged her to commemorate Peter Rempel's life in an icon and he gave it his blessing as a family icon. She prayerfully showed the icon to us, making us promise never to show the photograph we took of it, except in a context of devout prayer and worship. She honored him by painting a touching scene of the labor camp where he had selflessly protected the lives of others and died in the process. At the center of her depiction of the prison camp stands a tall figure of her father, hands raised to heaven as he offers his life to his Father.

Recently, Natasha's son, a young history student at Moscow University, had taken a trip to the region where his grandfather had perished in the Gulag. There, on the outskirts of the impoverished village, someone who still remembered the years of the camp's existence led her son to a lovely dense forest buried under winter snows. He was told that buried deep beneath the snow were countless multitudes of those who had never survived the ordeal of their imprisonment. This was the closest he came to visiting his grandfather's grave.

*Natasha Rempel, icon painter, in her Moscow home*

His mother, Natasha, was now divorced from his Russian father and had reclaimed her Mennonite name. But she had never identified again with the faith community of her youth, and was now a faithful member of the Russian Orthodox Church. However, she did say that she was happy to join our informal gatherings on Sunday afternoons as a link to her father's faith community. Our fellowship with her went very deep, to the very core of our shared faith. Though our religious expressions differed, our common Lord drew us together.

It seemed that behind all the stories of Mennonites who had accomplished a dramatic exodus from Russia, there always lurked another sadder story like these—the reality of the remnant who remained behind. Their stories were complex, shot through with heartache and tragedy. For us it meant that we felt more and more drawn to hear their experiences. We listened to their accounts of suffering in order to understand the whole tapestry of Mennonite life in Russia. And in our listening, the very act became a kind of sacrament of affirmation that validated their vital part in the total story. Indeed, the motif of suffering, so central to the Mennonite experience in Soviet Russia, linked them deeply with the profound mystery of suffering shared by countless millions of Russians of the twentieth century. It also connected them with their distant forebears of the Reformation period, the early Anabaptists of Europe, who had been persecuted for their faith, sealing their testimony with their blood.

*Peter P. Rempel, Mennonite minister who perished in a labor camp in Arkhangelsk*

I well remember the time we visited a remote former Mennonite village in Siberia, where we heard many stories of the years of oppression under Stalin. One old man, after recounting some of the experiences of his family, looked inquiringly deep into my face and asked, "Did the people in the West *know* what we were enduring in those years?" What could I answer, if my response was followed by a further probe as to why no one came to their rescue?

The experience of this village, ironically named Neudachino, meaning "not lucky" or unfortunate, was unique in that it had remained intact as a Mennonite community even through the years of persecution. We were visiting to ascertain what further help would be appropriate in its economic struggle at this challenging time. The trip took place over Christmas 1991, the year the Soviet Union began to crumble. We returned to Moscow to find a new regime was taking over; Yeltsin had triumphed over Gorbachev. The long journey on the Trans-Siberian Railway gave us ample time to meditate as the huge train rumbled over vast snowy wastes, pausing at times in remote railway stations where poor women sold us freshly cooked potatoes through the train windows.

We traveled with a dear Russian friend, Natasha, with whom we were doing some work in a Moscow publishing house, acting as advisors for the publication of Christian literature from the West. She was visiting her American fiancé, Jeff Busscher, in Novosibirsk, so had been glad to share the long journey. The several days and nights in the cramped quarters of the sleeping compartment were spent discussing a wide range of topics, including Russian literature and history, and most importantly, deepening our understanding of her newly found Russian Orthodox faith. Later in our time in Moscow, we had the unique experience of attending her Russian Orthodox wedding.

She slowly began trusting us more and more with her heart's concerns about her beloved Russia, as scenes of deprivation and poverty passed by our train windows day and night, interspersed by vast tracts of snow-covered wastes. I recall her teaching us a Russian song about a Christmas tree. We sang together as the long slow miles took us further from Moscow, where matters of a more serious nature were transpiring with the demise of Gorbachev.

Alighting from the train in Omsk in the early morning, we were met by a friendly looking young man from a Mennonite family named Neufeld, who had been dispatched to meet us and drive us to the village. We conversed in a mixture of Russian, German, and Low German. The latter would have been his preference, but was not ours! He took us straight to his parents' home in one of the simple houses in the broad street of the village that looked like any Mennonite village of the Ukraine. The house was humble and clean, and we were comfortably accommodated. However, the exercise of using an outhouse at 25 degrees below zero Celsius was a new challenge! It was strange to be welcomed into a tight community of people, all with names found in our Clearbrook telephone directory in Canada! Many spoke Low German and baked the same kind of *zwieback* (bread rolls) and *piroshki* (bread rolls filled with ground meat) eaten by their relatives in Canada. They fed us well during our time there and had clearly mastered the art of surviving the hardships of Soviet life.

*Russian Orthodox wedding of Natasha and Jeff Busscher, with Father Alexander Borisov officiating*

It was a unique experience to crowd into their little church, which met in a modest house adapted as a prayer house. It was an example of the kind of hybrid life lived by Mennonites in Russia today; they read the Bible in German, prayed and preached in Low German, and sang their hymns in Russian. The hymns were some of those we had learned in the Baptist Church that we attended in Moscow, with rich harmonies and minor keys. Such singing always conjured up for me the years of persecution and suffering.

We learned that the village had come to the attention of a prominent sociologist from the university in Novosibirsk, Natalia Baranova. She was fascinated by the contrast between their lifestyle and that of similar Russian villages around them. For example, she noted how a typical Russian village would kill a pig and devour it in short order, with the accompanying drinking and celebrations. However, the Mennonites would do the task in an orderly and disciplined manner, making sausage and lard to last them for a long time. She interpreted the difference as springing from their obvious connection to things Dutch as indicated by their names. But we knew that their lifestyle owed more to their recent past, with roots in the Mennonite traditions of the colonies in Ukraine.

Professor Baranova was also impressed with the cleanliness of Neudachino, with its clean floors and shoes at the door, compared to the typical Russian villages. She became a good friend and helper of the village, always a welcome visitor in their homes, and sometimes escorting other important figures and visitors.

The believers of the area had gone through hardships similar to the rest of the Mennonite population of the Soviet Union, except that they had not been forced into further exile to the Far East. The years of persecution had taken their toll on them with many succumbing to the harsh conditions of the forced labor camps in the *Trudarmia* (work army). Some of the women showed us the scars on their bodies caused by the brutal treatment they had received during those terrible years, deformed shoulders from hauling heavy loads of logs or crippled feet from standing for hours in freezing water. Their leader, Gerhard Neufeld, in whose home we stayed, had spent many years in prison more recently. He was raising a fine family of young people who followed his example of faith and frugality.

These believers were part of the wider network of "Jakob's kin," yet they had little in common with his learning or sophistication. But one thing they shared with him was their need to face again the perennial Mennonite dilemma—to stay or to leave. For just at that time, they were being wooed by the German government, under the laws of the repatriation of Russian citizens of German descent. The temptation to abandon their present homeland (which at this critical juncture might just be heading for some slight improvements!) for rosier material prospects elsewhere was the subject of constant conversation among the younger folk. Yet we soon learned that it was a topic strongly banned in the Neufeld house—Gerhard saw in it a temptation of biblical proportions. He bitterly complained that the only letters that reached them from those who had recently immigrated to Germany were full of stories about new cars and fridges, and contained no spiritual news about growth in the faith. As we followed the course of this debate over the next decade, we were to see his final capitulation at the end of his life when ill health overtook him. One by one his offspring succumbed, against all his pleading, wisdom, and prayers. Once again the fabric of Mennonite life was rent, and pain and misunderstanding followed.

*Worship service at a church in Neudachino, Omsk*

Yet we felt we had discovered a goldmine of personalities in Neudachino, and our bond with them would continue as they came to Moscow to visit us and to stay with us while their emigration papers were processed. They were even concerned for our welfare in the big city, wondering how we could possibly sustain ourselves! I well remember the time they arrived on the train after a journey of several days from Siberia. They brought with them a plastic pail full of flour, embedded with many eggs, plus other produce like butter and cheese from their own modest farms. We grew to love them and felt their deeply conflicted emotions. They were seeing the years of struggle to keep the faith and maintain their livelihood gradually ebbing away, only to be replaced by an unknown future in a wealthy distant land, whose language was their only connection to it.

In subsequent years MCC sent a very fine couple, Ben and Erna Falk, to Neudachino to assist the villagers in their economic struggle. Some significant improvements were developed, including a prosperous cheese factory. But eventually emigration won the day and the Mennonite presence diminished considerably, leaving the village to be inherited by their Russian neighbors. Later we heard about the younger generation who had immigrated to Germany and made a new life for themselves. They were grateful for all the material blessings and opportunities for their children. But many of them had a strange nostalgia for the harmony of their common life in the Siberian village and were haunted by a sense of loss, and a lingering question: "What might we have accomplished together, if we had persevered in Neudachino?"

One further contact with the scattered Mennonite family was occasioned by a trip to the distant Soviet Republic of Kyrgyzstan. Here yet another segment of Jakob's kin had survived indescribable hardships under the cruel communist regime, with many being lost to the extreme deprivation. Yet a small remnant had absorbed the evil intent of Stalin, choosing to see a higher purpose in their sufferings. Like Joseph in the Bible, they were able to confess that what was meant for evil, God had been able to turn around for good (Genesis 50:20). In the capital city of Bishkek, formerly known as Frunze, a Bible school was training young workers to share the faith with the local population, who were largely of a Moslem background. Against all odds, they were heroically persevering, undaunted by the many hardships they were encountering and convinced that their very survival was a tool in the hands of a benevolent God.

In later years back in Canada, it was our privilege to work for a group who would support these faithful Christians. But in the 1990s, our contact with them only served to make the point that not all was lost in the experience of extreme brutality that communism had meted out on these quiet peace-loving communities. Yes, a way of life had been destroyed, but gradually we were coming to see that in the scattered fragments, God was indeed weaving a deeper pattern of survival and usefulness that only eternity would fully reveal.

Another family whom we came to know, the Viktor Fasts, came through our home at the Mennonite Centre in Moscow on their way out to Germany. We had visited them in Karaganda, Kazakhstan, a depressed mining city that had once been home to a large thriving Mennonite/Baptist congregation of people exiled there by Stalin. Viktor Fast was a prominent leader in the once thriving Mennonite Brethren church of that city. He had also been given some responsibilities in the education system of the city, teaching some topics connected with religion and apologetics, and also helping young people in their resistance to the drug culture. He was highly respected and preached to his flock of the need to be faithful with the task of carrying the torch of faith into the uncertain future of a church where finally some freedom was beginning.

*Viktor Fast (center, with glasses and mustache) and his family, preparing to immigrate to Germany from Karaganda, Kazakstan*

Viktor came from an interesting family that embodied the Soviet Mennonites' adaptation to the challenges of culture.[19] There were three brothers in his family. The oldest was Willi, who left the faith and became a professor of science at Tomsk University. Then there was Viktor, who became a key church leader in Karaganda, and finally, Vasili, who became a Russian Orthodox priest. The two minister brothers continued to pray for Willi and eventually he came to faith and was baptized into the Russian Orthodox Church. However, as a result, Willi was demoted from his teaching role and became a janitor in the institute he had once served as a professor. After a time, he was reinstated and remained in Russia.

For Viktor, however, the heartbreaking day came when he had to acknowledge that one of his daughters could no longer live in the

---

[19] See also Walter Sawatsky, "Dying for What Faith? Martyrologies to Inspire and Heal or to Foster Christian Division?" *Conrad Grebel Review* 18/2 (2000): 49.

unhealthy coal mining city of Karaganda, due to serious allergies. The choice of emigration might be a lifeline for her. The day they came through Moscow, they lined up their few suitcases in our hall, the sum total of all their worldly possessions. It was clear they had little to take to their new beginning in Germany, apart from their sadness at leaving their mission field in Russia and their faith that life had yet something good to offer them in a new land.

Years later, while we were serving in Ukraine at the Mennonite Centre there, we were delighted to meet Viktor Fast again, as he came through with a tour group from the church he was leading in his new homeland, Germany. He still had a heart for those less fortunate brothers and sisters of the wider Mennonite family; he was still faithfully reaching out to those in Ukraine, Kazakhstan, and other parts of the former Soviet Union.

Every discovery of the far-flung Mennonite family only increased in us the sense of kinship with these people who had suffered so much for their chosen or imposed destiny of remaining in this difficult land. Yet all these people that we were meeting were experiencing a fresh rising of hope—somehow the tide was turning for those who had remained in Russia during the hardest period of their people's history. Was God somehow rewarding them for their longsuffering and fidelity?

One further example of this long faithfulness came to us one day in Moscow. Two sisters came to visit us, imploring our help in seeking to make contact with their father. They had been told that he lived somewhere in Canada. They had lost touch with him after he managed to escape to the West, leaving them with their mother alone in their Mennonite village. They told us how they had lived through years of great hardships. But all through those years, the photograph of their united family hung on the living room wall of their tiny Siberian home. And to her death, their mother remained faithful to her husband.

It was very hard for them to discover that their father—who ironically was living close to our home in Canada—was now remarried with a new family. For years he waited for news of his family, but had given them up for dead during the long silence in communication. While on a leave to Canada, we were able to make contact with him. We visited him in his small, frugal home in Clearbrook and found him to be very suspicious and fearful when we knocked on his door. He did finally agree to help his first family with the documents they needed from him, enabling them to immigrate to Germany. Yet he remained adamant that he was too fearful ever to be in contact with them again, lest the long arm of the KGB would reach into his place of refuge in Canada and disturb his hard-won peace and security.

*Maureen and Herb with two sisters searching for their father in Canada*

It was a moving moment for us back in our apartment in Moscow, when we delivered the papers to his daughters and made a telephone call back to Canada, enabling them to speak with their father for the first time in fifty years. Such moments were rewarding for us, and we were thankful that in a small way we could provide a link and help people like these resolve some of the problems of their troubled past.

One day a young woman came to the Centre, telling us that she had an uncle living in the Okanagan Valley of British Columbia. She knew his name, but nothing more about him. We made several inquiries on her behalf and eventually she was able to make contact with him. He invited his niece to come and visit him in that beautiful part of Canada, where he had lived for many years since leaving Russia. After the young woman returned from her trip, I was a little anxious about how the experience would have impacted her. Did she resent her uncle's prosperity? Would she now be restless until she could go and live there, too? But when I asked her how she felt, her reply was touching. She said, "I was grateful to be able to meet my relatives. And I was glad that somewhere on the earth people can live in such happiness!"

One woman who liked to come to our gatherings at the Mennonite Centre was one of the first friends we made in Russia. Her name was Natalie, the wife of an army officer named Sergey. She was a teacher at the school next door to our first apartment on the outskirts of Moscow. She had no Mennonite connection, but was curious about our faith. She enjoyed practicing her English on us and helped us with our beginnings in Russian. The friendship developed over our years in Moscow, even when we moved into the apartment that housed the Centre.

*Maureen and Herb with Natalie (left) and Sergey (right) in Moscow*

Natalie represented the element in Soviet society that had been totally brainwashed with anti-Christian ideas. But she was suspicious that she was being deceived and wanted our help in getting at the truth. She was very reluctant to come to the Baptist Church we attended, being still uneasy about the propaganda she'd heard: that Baptists drink the blood of children! She earnestly asked us whether that was actually true! One cannot underestimate the struggle of those firmly entrenched in atheism as they tried to reach out to a new faith.

Natalie did finally summon the courage to come to church one Sunday. She understood that we prayed for particular needs there, and she came with a specific request. Her husband, the army officer, had lost a key which was somehow very important for his work responsibilities in Moscow. She felt God had heard her prayer when the key was found. She later attended our meetings at the Centre, where she met people with Mennonite connections. For a person raised under the protection of the Soviet military caste, it was an exposure to a totally different side of the Soviet story. In her own time, she eventually embraced the Christian faith and joined a small evangelical fellowship in the suburb of Moscow where she lived.

The Moscow Mennonite Centre where we served had a short life as the work of MCC in the former Soviet Union eventually moved to Ukraine. But the lives of those who passed through the Centre's doors hold a critical place in the story of the Mennonite people in Russia.

## One More Martyr: Alexander Men

There is one further aspect of our time in Moscow which deserves attention. We spent five years in Moscow, albeit with some breaks due to my shoulder injury, and our work there had been varied. Our discovery of our own family history was totally unexpected and our meetings with "trace" Mennonites were often surprising and meaningful, as we discovered a deep fellowship with people who sometimes hardly knew anything about the faith of their forebears. Yet there was another dimension that increasingly drew our attention. It came in the form of a deepening encounter with the suffering of Russian believers from other parts of the body of Christ. And it opened the door to a new understanding of the traditional faith of the Russian people, the Russian Orthodox Church.

We had come to Moscow as Mennonites with a particular history, and a desire to be of service to any remnant of our own people that we might meet. Yet the more we got to know people of faith in the city, the more we discovered a common bond of suffering that transcended the walls that have traditionally separated the groups of believers making up the wider faith community of Russia. The very experience of suffering, we realized, had a way of breaking down those walls and unifying those from very different religious groups.

It is a well-known fact, documented by writers like Aleksandr Solzhenitsyn in his book *The Gulag Archipelago*, that in the forced labor camps, Baptists, Adventists, Mennonites, Russian Orthodox, and many others found in one another brothers and sisters of a common faith. It was a great leveling, allowing essentials to surface and differences to be minimized. Mennonites who died for the faith were but a small segment of those who shed their blood as martyrs during Stalin's terrible purges.

It seemed to us that during our sojourn in Moscow, we were being drawn into that deeper fellowship, acknowledging that greater "noble company of martyrs." Our Anabaptist heritage had prepared us to recognize such sacrificial lives wherever we found them. Thousands of Russian Orthodox priests were sent to the Gulag or executed by Stalin's firing squads. Before the Revolution, we learned that there were over a thousand monasteries in Russia. Their destruction occasioned countless murders, incarcerations, and banishments. Baptist and Adventist pastors and leaders shared the same fate. Women who dared to teach their children the Bible were torn from their homes and sent to Siberia, leaving their small children uncared for, sometimes for years. And the leader of the Protestant publishing house, also a Baptist, spent several years in prison for leading an energetic youth group that met in his home, or in the forests surrounding Moscow.

Thus it was of great interest to us when, through our work with the Protestant publishing house, we were introduced to a fascinating circle of Russian Orthodox believers called the Hosanna Club. They comprised a number of recent young converts to the faith, including several former Jews. Their leaders, Andrei and Karina Cherniak, also Messianic Russian Jews, became close friends who invited us to their fellowship. We were surprised to discover another bond with them in that Rev. Michael Harper—the man who had prayed with us for a deeper life in the Spirit nearly thirty years ago in England—had also become a close friend of theirs and had prayed for them, too.

It was moving to enter the room where they met, to see their simple circular gathering with a cross and icon as focus. Andrei's beautiful guitar playing, and the occasional flute or violin, accompanied their songs, many of which they had written themselves. Their worship and testimonies were touching, and their fellowship warm and welcoming. We sensed the presence of the same Christ whom we had come to Moscow to serve. Yet this "happening in Moscow" was revealing Him to us in unexpected ways.

Our reading had encouraged us to take a fresh look at some of the traditions of Russian Orthodox Christianity like icons and candles that people such as ourselves had often condemned as empty ritual. We were challenged by Erika's sense of being consoled by such things. We learned from Russian Orthodox theologians to see icons as windows through which to view the person of Christ. As we did so, we became less troubled by the presence of icons, and more able to welcome them as aids to focus on Him. The worship of the Hosanna Club became a new experience of worship for us and we sensed the genuineness of its piety and its practical expression of faith.

We learned that many of the group had been disciples of Alexander Men, the brilliant Russian Orthodox priest who had been assassinated shortly before we arrived in Moscow. Our friend, Natasha Rempel, the icon painter, had been a member of his congregation. We came to recognize in this dynamic group of young people a kind of fresh discipleship that felt very close to the spirit of the early Anabaptists. They were zealous in their spiritual devotion to Jesus, and active in visiting the sick and poor of the city, of whom there were many.

One of the girls told me that they had discovered an elderly woman in one of the Moscow apartments that they visited. She had been a university lecturer, but now could not survive on her meager pension. They found her sick and starving, lying on a bed of old newspapers. She was very grateful for the care and help they brought her. It seems that there were all too many such cases for a city that claimed to be creating a new future of prosperity for its citizens.

It seemed to us that this energetic group of young people epitomized the kind of compassion and caring ministry that Mennonites had once been known for in Russia. In the 1990s, Russia was being inundated with teams of well-meaning Christians from the West sincerely bent on "bringing Christ to Russia," since the Soviet Union was finally falling apart and the door was opening for such activities. But to us it seemed Christ was already here in the quiet service of these young Russian Orthodox believers.

This fact was never more evident when, on one special occasion, they invited the renowned Canadian Roman Catholic, Jean Vanier, a personal friend of Alexander Men, to come and give a talk in a local auditorium on his work of caring for the mentally challenged. The young people invited families from all across the city to bring their handicapped family members to the gathering. They came from apartments where they had been hidden for a lifetime, with very little social support and next to no facilities. Many were carried in the arms of loved ones because Moscow had few wheelchairs at that time. It was a moving experience to see the compassion of young people and caring relatives affirmed by this humble man, Jean Vanier, as they sat and listened to his message of hope in the midst of suffering, their arms draped affectionately around their needy charges. The scene seemed to say, the compassionate Jesus of the Gospels is alive in Russia for those who will see Him in unexpected places.

The priest of the Russian Orthodox Church that these young people attended, the church of St. Cosmos and St. Damian in central Moscow, was Father Alexander Borisov. He had grown up with Alexander Men and later became part of Men's congregation, inheriting the mantle of leadership of the grieving congregation after their leader's death. Father Borisov welcomed us warmly into their circle and led a very lively evening Bible study that included believers from many different church backgrounds, including Baptist and Mennonite.

Shortly before our coming to Moscow, the Protestant publishing house had organized a Christian rally where the featured speaker was Alexander Men. It was a truly ecumenical gathering. Those who attended were deeply shocked at his death soon after the rally. He died on September 9, 1990. We arrived in Moscow in October of that year. Outrage at his death was fresh in the minds of those whom we met through our work. As we tried to learn more about his life, we were more and more impressed with his role as a spiritual leader in the Russian religious landscape, and the hope it promised for the future of Christian faith in Russia.[20]

Alexander Men was born on January 20, 1935, to a devout Russian Orthodox mother, herself a convert from Judaism. His grandmother had experienced a dramatic healing as a young woman through the ministry of John of Kronstadt, an eminent Russian Orthodox saint. Alexander was baptized at seven months in the banned Catacombs Orthodox Church, a segment of the Russian Orthodox Church that refused to cooperate with the Soviet authorities. As a young child, he was unusually devout and heard the call to the religious life very young. He studied biology at an institute in Moscow that was relocated to Irkutsk Siberia, but he was not allowed to graduate due to anti-Semitic prejudice. He studied theology at the Leningrad Theological Seminary, graduating in 1960. He was ordained first as a deacon and then to the priesthood while still a young man. In keeping with the custom of the Russian Orthodox Church, he was allowed to remain married.

---

[20] See Yves Hamant, *Alexander Men: A Witness for Contemporary Russia (A Man for Our Times)* (Torrance, Calif.: Oakwood Publications, 1995).

*Father Alexander Men (1935–1990)*

Men became a prolific author. His most famous book, *Son of Man*, was a bestseller and introduced thousands of Russians to Jesus at a time when many of them were totally ignorant of Him. The small humble church where he carried out his ministry, Novaya Derevnya, became a focal point for many seeking faith and an understanding heart to listen to their problems. He baptized thousands and was a popular figure in the media. He helped found the Russian Bible Society in cooperation with other Christians in Moscow, which also earned him the disapproval of some strict Russian Orthodox believers. He worked tirelessly as priest and mentor to the hundreds who made the pilgrimage to his home and church. He was a friend of many distinguished intellectuals like Aleksandr Solzhenitsyn and Nadezhda Mandelstam, to whom he gave final rites before she died.

His brutal murder occurred while he was making his way through the woods from his home village of Semkhoz to Novaya Derevnya in order to celebrate the liturgy. The character of his death—an axe blow to the neck—is the traditional Russian method of assassination used by anti-Semites. It also implied his identification with believers outside the strict confines of the Russian Orthodox Church; he had become an offence to the hierarchy of the church. The church and the KGB were suspected in his death, but no one has ever been charged with his murder. Like the Anabaptists, and his Savior, Men taught forgiveness of enemies.

It is here that we find the connection to the subject of this book. Alexander Men was more than a Russian Orthodox priest.[21] He was part of Russia's army of martyrs, and as such is vitally linked to the Mennonite martyrs of Russia. He was also one of the countless—probably millions—who were slaughtered during those bloody years of persecution, injustice, and brutality that the Mennonite people also endured. He is a figure who unites all those like Jakob and his kin, who came to an untimely end at the hands of that brutal regime.

It is also significant that Erika, the daughter of a man who was raised in a community where Anabaptist faith and values were taught and cherished, should later in life find inspiration and comfort from the writings and example of Alexander Men. She would find herself much closer to this church that still honors Men and his teaching, than to her father's church that seemed by now so remote to her. In recent years, she reported visiting this church again and enjoying talks with Alexander Borisov, the current priest. Is it not the same Jesus that shines through?

We count it a privilege that during our five years in Moscow we were able to meet with those who were the spiritual progeny of this great man of faith, Alexander Men, and that in a small way we could support Erika and others in their search for a way to make some sense of their own trials and experiences. Through no fault of their own, many people of faith—from various church traditions—suffered immeasurable losses. According to Tertullian, the second-century theologian, "The blood of the martyrs is the seed of the church." May that seed be multiplied a hundredfold on the soil of the former Soviet Union.

---

[21] See Herb Klassen and Maureen Klassen, "An Evangelical in the Russian Orthodox Church: Fr. Alexander Men (1935–1990)" *Direction* 26/1 (Spring 1997): 30–42; and Maureen Klassen, "Fr. Men and John 17," presented at the Alexander Men Summer Conference, Drew University, 1998 (www.alexandermen.com).

# 8

# To the Depths

A Russian once quizzed me about our experience in Russia and our acquaintance with its life and the culture. "Ah, but have you traveled to the depths?" he asked me, and left me to interpret the meaning of this cryptic comment.

As I have reflected on it over the years, I have realized that no matter how many concerts we attend, books we read, films we watch, and museums and galleries we visit, these are nothing in comparison to one visit to a Russian dacha or an invitation to stay overnight or longer in a Russian home.

Furthermore, one will never penetrate to the depths of a culture until one has listened to the people give an account of their suffering in their native tongue. This is what I understand as *going to the depths*.

We deeply valued all our contacts with former or "trace" Mennonites. But we particularly desired to be in touch with any related to our own family who had endured some of the difficult times and experiences. That desire was fulfilled when we were contacted by some relatives in Canada telling us that we should visit a family in Crimea, Garri and Lilya Klassen. Garri Klassen was a distant relative of CF's, and a native of Jakob's Crimea. Garri had been exiled to Kazahkstan as a young man with his family after the Revolution. They had only in recent years been able to return to their beloved Crimea. Our first contact came with the two sons of this couple who, we were told, would be in Moscow on a certain date and would be happy to come and see us at our apartment.

It so happened that on that particular day our telephone line was dead and we were not able to receive a ring on the phone. What could we do since the two men had told us that they would call us as soon as they arrived in town? I joked with my husband—should we just pick up the receiver on and off during the day and see if anyone was there? I did this once, and was shocked to hear a voice on the line say, "This is Vadim Klassen calling."

Was it more than a coincidence that I had lifted the receiver at that exact moment? I told this story to a Russian once and he remarked, "This is not unusual in Russia. You in the West are so used to organization and structure. Here in Russia we live by our instincts and intuition much more. We still don't have a telephone directory in Moscow," which I also knew to my frustration! "Such coincidences are the stuff of life here."

So we duly met the two young men and they strongly encouraged us to visit their parents in Crimea. Our connection with them marked a milestone in our Russian sojourn in more ways than one. In my study of the language, it had been my deep desire to reach the point where I could hear the stories of Russian people in their own heart language. Many times in our contacts with people, much was lost in translation and one was left with a sense that one hadn't really got to the heart of their experience. That trip to Crimea was the first time we were able to hear someone pour out their heart in the Russian language and to feel that we were understanding.

That trip is also indelibly etched in my memory because of an experience I had on the journey to Crimea. It was an experience that in a strange way connected me to countless travelers in Russia who have seen their life's hopes and dreams dashed forever in one specific irrevocable moment of destiny. In particular, it was somehow linked to some of the nightmare experiences of separation and loss that tended to come to mind if one reflected that we were traveling on the same railway that had been the scene of many tragic moments for the Mennonite people. I recalled one story I had heard about a large family who was emigrating—they lost a daughter in the railway station. When the father offered to go and look for her, the terrified mother forbade him saying, "I can't lose my husband as well as a daughter!" Fortunately for all, when the train got underway, the daughter was found on board!

This is what happened to me, also in a railway station, at the beginning of our journey to Crimea. It was early spring in Moscow when we decided to take the trip to visit our relatives in Crimea. The weather was still cool in the capital, though we expected the time in Crimea close to the Black Sea would be warmer and so we didn't pack our winter clothes or wear winter jackets. I was wearing an extra sweater, but Herb had only a light summer jacket to shield him against what proved to be a very chilly Moscow early morning as we arrived at the railway station. We dragged our luggage across the huge railway station and under a long dark tunnel, finally arriving at the correct platform for our train. It was about an hour before the train was due to depart, so no train had arrived yet and we were forced to wait for it out on a very breezy platform.

After about half an hour, my husband decided he needed a restroom, but of course there was none in the vicinity. So he left me with all the baggage on the chilly platform, while he retraced his steps a good way across the vast railway station and through the dark tunnel alone, back to the last place he had seen the washroom sign. I was somewhat anxious for him, but thought he'd be his usual nimble self and return in a very short time.

The minutes went by as I watched the huge clock on the platform nearing the time of our train's departure. Still no train! But also, no husband! Finally, about ten minutes before its departure time, the huge train lumbered down the tracks onto the platform.

The assembled awaiting passengers hastily gathered up their luggage and started boarding. This usually long and slow procedure was hurried due to the lateness of the train's arrival. Swiftly the platform was emptying as the passengers found their seats. My anxiety was mounting as I realized that my husband had the tickets and I couldn't move all the luggage alone. I would have to wait for his appearance. My eyes were fixed on the staircase where he would appear, but no sign of him.

I knew the routine trip to the bathroom should never have taken this long. Had he become sick? Or disoriented and lost? Or had someone, recognizing him as a foreigner, attacked him and robbed him in that dark tunnel? Or were there more sinister options? This was still Russia, and many dark deeds were still happening to foreign visitors. My imagination began to spin. It was as if I suddenly made connection with the many Mennonite people who had been tossed around upon this continent, meeting and departing in railway stations like this.

How many people had lost each other in hostile crowds never to meet again? And how many arrests had been made just at the point when people had been ready to embark on a new and liberating chapter of their lives? With a sickening feeling I realized that Herb had all our money, and even our passports.

The train was almost ready to depart, and by this time I was becoming frantic as I stood paralyzed on the platform in the cold morning breeze. But suddenly, just as I was giving up all hope, a figure appeared at the top of the staircase in an unfamiliar light-colored well-padded jacket. He rushed to my side, whisked up the bulk of the baggage, telling me to grab the rest. We made a dash for the nearest door, getting in just before the train began to move out of the station.

It was a while before we could make our way through the cars to the right location for our reservations and as I followed him along the corridor I was mystified at his change of attire. Finally, we located our places and I sank into my seat—and began to cry. It was some time before it dawned on my bewildered husband that his wife might have been just a little anxious. Especially since his course of action seemed so eminently logical. After visiting the washroom, he had decided to check out a couple of kiosks in the main terminal to buy a warmer jacket! A good move, he felt, with the chilly weather! And since the train wasn't in yet, it seemed the right thing to do! By this time in his narration, I was a nervous wreck, weeping profusely—partly from frustration, but mainly from an immense sense of relief that no harm had befallen my spouse. The train was by now lumbering through the suburbs of Moscow. We were on our way and all was well.

I felt that in those moments of panic and anxiety, I had touched a common place that all of us who are sojourners share. Some travelers in the midst of a journey do fall by the wayside. I recalled the many stories of Mennonite people who were attacked, arrested, separated from loved ones, or denied their dreams. Many of them had gathered in railway stations, expectantly waiting for a journey to a new life, only to be turned back to a life of deprivation and suffering. We take our fate in our hands when we travel this world's highways, railroads, and oceans. "Have a safe trip," is no ordinary platitude. We take our lives in our hands every time we venture forth; but as people of faith, we find strength by placing them in the Lord's hands.

## The Visit to Crimea

The long train journey to Crimea took us many hours as the large Russian train rumbled across Russia and Ukraine for three days, revealing the interesting difference between the rambling style of the rundown villages of Russia and the more orderly ones of Ukraine.

When we arrived, we were met by Garri Klassen, a large, good-looking man, white-haired now after his long arduous career in medicine as a burn specialist. Now his health was failing him. With his sons he had built a lovely little home in Stary Krim, an ancient city in the interior of Crimea. It felt more like a dacha with its shady courtyard. Under the fruit trees we ate outside in the cool of the evening.

We sat together with Garri and Lilya, day after day, listening to Garri's life story. He poured it out to us in what had become the language of his heart, the Russian language. At times, it's true, he did lapse into Low German or High German, but Russian was the language that captured for him the core of what he had suffered. We felt deeply privileged to listen to him and to hear him in that tongue.

*Garri Klassen outside the home he built in Stary Krim, Crimea*

Every day we sat on a sofa in his tiny living room with Garri sitting on a chair facing us as if to deliver an important speech demanding intense concentration. Often his narrative paused as he broke into tears about his experiences during the hard early days of his exile to Kazahkstan in 1941. His story was punctuated by hand gestures that grew more intense for words like "repressed" and "executed," words used in the description of the oppressive years under Stalin.

Garri had grown up as an atheist and had nearly died during the years of his family's exile to Kazakhstan. He told us how he had been left for dead, lying beside the road in a certain town where many were dying of typhus. Miraculously, a woman had come along and somehow helped him to get to the local hospital, where he had been treated and slowly revived.

He told us of the years of deprivation, living in primitive structures called *semlyankas* or dugouts, with no amenities of any kind. These were little more than holes in the ground, covered with any material at hand, like branches, earth, and odd scraps of metal. After years of hardship, working by day in a factory and studying by night, he eventually managed to study medicine. He had done well under the communist system. Becoming a qualified burn specialist, he eventually achieved a fairly prosperous life. However, at one point he reached a crisis in his own personal life, something which ultimately led to his embrace of the Christian faith later in life. His wife was a Russian woman who had only recently come to faith through reading a book by Josh McDowell, *Only a Carpenter*. They represented much that was good in Russian culture.

Garri had an older sister, Hedy, who lived nearby in an impoverished but orderly old house with a fabulous garden. She grew beautiful flowers and luscious vegetables, but lived a very austere hand-to-mouth life as a widow. She could have fit into our hometown in Canada, with her simple life and modest demeanor. She had endured a very hard life and supplemented her meager pension by collecting fruit for a collective farm, which sometimes paid her scantily in kind with nuts or surplus fruit. She told us that as a young girl, before the Revolution, she had attended the Mennonite high school in Spat, a sister school to the one in Karassan that Jakob and his brothers and also CF had attended. After the exile in Kazakhstan, she returned to Crimea, following Garri and Lilya. She did not profess any faith and spent a lot of her time consumed with anxiety about her subsistence and the fate of her mentally handicapped son. She would later also immigrate to Germany with her brother Garri, where she continued her frugal life as a pensioner, caring for her handicapped son. It seemed that all that she had been through had severed any ties she had with her childhood faith.

One felt a kind of sadness for these people—Garri, Lilya, Hedy, and the countless others—and yet we could not but admire their courageous lives and wonder whether prosperity in Canada would have been more character-forming. (Later we were saddened by the news that Garri and Lilya had trouble finding their way in the faith context of their newly adopted homeland, Germany, viewing many of the contemporary churches as too superficial after all that they had endured.) As we deepened our relationship with Garri and his family, we found a meaningful bond with them developing. They in turn let us know how valuable it was for them to be granted a link with the part of the family that called Canada home.

Once, when Garri's son, Vadim, and his wife, Olga, came to Moscow, we went together to a performance of the play *Vospominania* (Remembrances), by Sholem Asch. It is the original story behind the popular musical *Fiddler on the Roof*. How poignant to see the archetypal story of this Russian village presented to a Russian audience, in a cultural context where the actual sufferings of such times are graphic and realistically remembered.

*Vadim and Olga Klassen with Maureen and Herb Klassen in Moscow*

As we gained a fuller understanding of how the decades of communism had affected this family, we felt we were being prepared for getting to know Erika and her circle. There was a deepening of our understanding of what forces had formed the experience of those who lived through the years of the Soviet reality.

Part of our acceptance of their life and experiences involved opening ourselves to what they viewed as positive in their Russian culture. It seemed they were saying that it was not all bad, and that they had found much of value in spite of all the negative influences. We were happy to allow them to host us in this journey of discovery. They introduced us to the work of famous folk singer and poet, Bulat Okuzhava, and the renowned singer, Anna German. It was fascinating to learn that this woman, one of Russia's most famous singers, had Mennonite roots.

Anna German had sung some of the most beautiful Russian songs in her many concert appearances. Garri had once attended one of her concerts and was surprised when she suddenly broke into a simple German song, *Gott ist die Liebe* (God is Love). When asked where she learned it, she replied, "At my grandmother's knee of course!" It turned out she was related to a Martens family from Melitopol in Ukraine, and came by her considerable musical talent by way of the Mennonite heritage so dear to Garri himself. I have a much cherished CD, one that includes the hauntingly beautiful rendering of the song running through all my reflections about Mary and Jakob—the song by Lermontov about the traveler alone on the highway.

## The Aivazovsky Painting

During one of our visits to Crimea, Garri took us to Feodosia. There we saw the art gallery dedicated to the artist Ivan Aivazovsky (1817–1900), Russia's most famous seascape painter. We enjoyed seeing the gathered work of this local artist whose work also hangs in the prestigious galleries of Moscow and St. Petersburg. At the time, I did not realize that this artist had an unusual connection to Mary and Jakob—a connection that would only become evident years later.

This connection involves a painting that has come down to us through the years and has special unfinished significance for our family. I believe it may be the last gift that Jakob had a part in bequeathing to his Canadian descendants. The painting hung for years in CF and Mary's home. Mary gave it to Harold once on his birthday, but never explained how she procured it. Nor did she mention anything about his father when she gave it to him. The picture always hung in a special place of honor in their home. It depicts in fine detail, a beautiful seaport of the kind painted many times by this world-renowned artist. It closely resembles other paintings in a book that is in our possession, given to us by Garri, depicting seaports of the Black Sea and Mediterranean region.

*Lilya, Maureen, and Garri Klassen at the Aivazovsky Art Gallery in Feodosia*

While home in Abbotsford on a leave from our work in Moscow, we were looking at the picture with Harold and Ruthie. We turned the picture to the back and read Mary's carefully typed note: "This picture is by Ivan Aivazovsky." We were shocked to see the renowned artist's name written there, not having noticed before the small initials, IA, at the bottom left of the painting. We also have no idea how it was procured. Because she gave it to Harold, it seems possible that Mary acquired it through her first husband, Jakob, since he was a native of Crimea. Maybe during the turbulent times of the Revolution such items were traded for other goods or services. It might even have been traded for produce from the Mennonite farms at a time of need and famine when food was a priority. It is good to know that this Aivazovsky painting is safe with Jakob's descendants in Canada.

## More Reflections

In all our trips to Crimea during our five years in Moscow, we never thought of making a visit to the old Mennonite village of Karassan, where CF had gone to school and where Jakob had grown up. We even wondered whether Aunt Greta, with whom CF stayed during his school years, might have been a relative on Garri's side of the family. Pursuing that part of the Mennonite tapestry would have to wait until another period in Ukraine five years later (and another Mennonite Centre!), when we would pick up more threads.

Garri greatly appreciated our friendship, and many other visits with him and his family in Russia were to follow. His family's choice to remain in Russia after the Revolution had cost him dearly. And though his mother had been a woman of faith, the years under communism had taken their toll on his own grasp of the faith of his forebears. He had been well treated by the authorities in his pursuit and practice of medicine as a burn specialist. He had not compromised his integrity, but neither had he spoken about his background. It was only after the "cultural thaw" of the Khrushchev era (1953–1964), when Russian writers who had been suppressed began to publish again, that he voluntarily returned to his faith. At the time of our meeting, he and his wife were active in the Baptist Church in Crimea. Only one of his sons followed in his steps, though both of them had done well educationally, one being also a medical doctor and one a designer for the Lada automobile factory in Tagliatti.

In the late 1990s, when life became unbearably difficult for them in Russia, they immigrated to Germany. Garri it seemed had accepted the price he had paid for his family's choice not to flee to Canada years earlier, though he regretted the lost opportunities for his sons. Garri had heard about C.F. Klassen, but never met him. He met Erika once in Moscow, but had no great feeling of affinity with her. The Mennonite bonds were too tenuous for either of them. Yet for me Garri was part of that thinly spun web of relationships that marked him as one of Jakob's kin—one of those whose lives were inextricably bound together as part of the tapestry of suffering that linked them to the larger Mennonite story.

Our encounters with Jakob's kin were truly the opportunity to touch the depths of something that struck me again when reading *Hope Abandoned* by Nadezhda Mandelstam, the widow of the famous Russian-Jewish poet, Osip Mandelstam. As few others have done, she tries to plumb the deep meaning of the suffering of the Russian people. She believes that the extreme cruelty inflicted upon the population was a kind of desecration of all that it once held holy and good, like marriage, family, national institutions, and faith.[22] How does a people group conquer such destruction of all that they hold dear? Is it, as in the case of many, by escaping? Or is the very endurance of those sufferings also a kind of triumph? She suggests that in adhering to

---

[22] Mandelstam, *Hope Abandoned: A Memoir*, 347.

those values, even at the cost of great deprivation and ultimately death itself, a people through their long endurance can offer their sufferings as a kind of sacrament.

Many of the Mennonite people who remained soon fell victim to brutality, starvation, cruel working conditions, and to the depression so often associated with communist repression. They did not feel in the least heroic about their ordeal and many of them, understandably, questioned their God and their faith in the worst years of their hardships. Countless of them died terrible deaths, including many innocent children and victimized women. Some of the more pious among them sought to make sense of the ordeal with sentiments like Job's utterance: "Shall we receive good at the hand of the Lord and not receive evil?" (Job 2:10). And it is true that such yieldedness (Anabaptist *Gelassenheit*) lay at the core of the faith that had guided them down through the years. For some who survived the labor camps, there is no doubt that something of that stoic faith and endurance sometimes made the difference between those who persevered and those who succumbed.

People like Garri and his family represent the many thousands whose stories are currently being written or may still come to light, as more access is given to records and more relatives research and tell the experiences of their loved ones. We owe them our attention as just tribute to the fact that the evil of cruel totalitarian regimes never has the last word, as long as those who suffer do not allow that evil to define who they are and what they believe. They triumph through their very refusal to deny their faith, their humanity, and their God.

In the final analysis, however, the dark colors of this tapestry are a part of the mystery of suffering that will never receive a simple explanation in this life. We can only applaud the longsuffering endurance of the Russian Mennonite people, weep with those who experienced immeasurable loss, and rejoice with those who were able to put together some semblance of new life after the storm passed. These 20th-century witnesses give testimony, just as their Anabaptist forebears did, by their very suffering. We who come after them must honor their journey and recognize that they also are a critical thread in the larger Russian Mennonite story. And we recognize, too, that Mennonites were not the only ones who suffered in this way. A huge multitude of Russian citizens were arrested, imprisoned, and later died or were executed during Stalin's great purge of Russian society; while impossible to know exactly, some scholars put the number at twenty million.[23] All who suffered in the "Great Terror" of the "Soviet Inferno" share a common bond.

---

[23] Letkemann, "The Great Terror," 36.

# 9

# Return to Moscow in 1994

Our years in Moscow spanned a time of great upheaval for the people of Russia. With them, we lived through some of the most dramatic changes since the time of the Revolution. As noted earlier, on December 26, 1991, the Soviet Union was formally dissolved. The declaration acknowledged the independence of the Republics, creating the Commonwealth of Independent States. On the evening before, the Soviet flag was lowered from the Kremlin and replaced with the Russian tricolor. These changes spelled the end of the Soviet Union as it had been known for over seventy years.

By all accounts, the collapse of the USSR was one of the most sudden and dramatic territorial losses experienced by any state in history. Between 1990 and 1992, the Kremlin lost direct control over about one-third of the Soviet territory that it once held. In our experience, the collapse of the Soviet Union led, at first, to an influx of goods and services that had been unavailable previously. The new economic opportunities were welcomed by our friends. But gradually, the gap between the rich and poor widened. Many suffered severe losses as the economic crisis deepened.

The transition was also not without fatalities. During the crises of October 1993, first at the Ostankino TV station, and then with the barricading of the Russian White House, there were more than 200 casualties. At such times, we stayed at home in our apartment watching the events on CNN. It was a tense time. We heard rumors of so-called "bread vans" driving to the back of the White House and removing bodies from inside the besieged building. Was Russia descending into chaos, we wondered? Was there more bloodshed in store?

We tried to continue our normal life as quietly as possible. I remember being relieved when the advent of a new constitution seemed to bring hope of more stability.

# Return to Moscow in 1994

More troubles were ahead for Russia with the start of the war against Chechnya, the economic ups and downs, and Yeltzin's erratic leadership style. Many saw him as the savior of Russia, but others were slower to put their trust in his promise of a new day. Erika seemed to maintain a sober view of all these affairs. She had lost faith in the political rollercoaster of power games. She remained rather cynical about her homeland's aspirations.

The new Commonwealth of Independent States proved to be a transitional reality, but it was exciting to watch as one by one the various Republics declared their independence from Moscow, and then tried to revive their different ethnicities. Though raw nationalism could prove to be a violent cause, we could not help but rejoice to see people again singing their native songs and doing their national dances. Yet the struggle would prove to be an ongoing one, lasting many years and combined with much economic instability. We hoped that the changes unfolding all around us would have some long-lasting effects on the political climate and on the way of life for our newfound relative, Erika, and her family.

With the declaration of new economic opportunities and a free market economy, many from Western countries rushed in to help Russians realize their dreams of a new prosperity. Our involvement with some in the Russian business community gave us insight into how they were impacted by these efforts. At a conference we attended, I chatted with a woman who doubted that foreigners could teach former Soviet citizens much about hard work and frugality, given all that the Russians had endured. She was especially disappointed to learn that one busload of tourists had bribed their bus driver to take them to Moscow's *McDonalds*, even though it was not part of their tour itinerary. She seemed to have a deep sense of what was ethically correct. She began to question me more about the religious underpinnings of our work, but finally said, "What you are talking about interests me greatly. But we've lived a lifetime under Soviet rule and cannot respond to these things. That part of us that should respond was destroyed by all the years of communism."

I assured her that I did not see her that way. I was too impressed by her innate sense of morality and values. But she smilingly deferred, saying: "Please talk to my children. It is not too late for them."

She reminded me of Erika and how the years under Soviet rule had shaped her. We sincerely hoped that she would be able to experience some of the greater freedoms Gorbachev had promised and that Yeltsin was seeking to implement. But most of all, we wished that she could add to her deep sense of right and wrong by embracing something of the faith of her father's community.

*Maureen with Erika and Oleg in Herb and Maureen's Moscow apartment*

However, Erika was a cynic at heart as a result of all that her family had endured. She had few expectations of the volatile scene swirling around us. Her perspective proved to be realistic. Very little would ever change for Erika and Oleg in any material way. But what had changed was the stranglehold that the KGB had on the documents she was seeking to access. Finally, information became available that would fill in the gaps of our understanding of what had become of Jakob Reimer, information that once seemed forever lost to us and to the relatives of countless Mennonites and other Russians.

On November 6, 1994, we returned to Moscow, after receiving five months of treatment in Canada for my injured shoulder. We were finishing our term of service in Moscow and planned to resume our life in British Columbia in summer 1995. Because our work at the Mennonite Centre was concluding, we needed to relocate to yet another apartment, the fifth in our Moscow sojourn. But we were eager to reconnect with all the individuals who still needed our help and encouragement.

During this time, Herb had been able to pursue some meaningful connections with a prison ministry in some of the notoriously overcrowded prisons in the Moscow area. This was a work close to his heart from his years as a prison chaplain in Canada.

And of course, we were especially looking forward to arranging for Erika to visit us in Canada when we were back in British Columbia.

Erika was aware that Harold, after his visit to Moscow, had been diagnosed with cancer and might not have too long to live. Her anticipated visit in summer 1995 took on even more significance. She would now have to face losing him for the second time, after such a brief acquaintance.

Since our first meeting with Erika, the mighty changes that had happened in the land of her birth meant that, for her, travel might finally be an option. She was quite certain that her husband, Oleg, who had been a rocket scientist under the Soviet regime, would never be allowed to travel abroad. The great political changes under Yeltsin were a strange mixture.

As we sat on the plane in November 1994, we were anxious to see just how deep and far-reaching those changes would prove to be.

Ironically, the inflight movie on the transatlantic flight was *Awakenings*. It is the story of a man suffering from a severe mental condition that cuts him off from all normal life and interaction. An exceptional treatment sets him free from his malady and he begins to approximate normalcy. The parallel was graphic for me. I contemplated the huge reality of the Soviet Union and its peoples, submerged for decades under the brutal cloud of communism, "awakened" to new possibilities and a new life. As the man gradually sinks back into his debilitating condition, the film communicates the palpable fear that the awakening will be short-lived and not sustainable.

As the plane approached Moscow and I reflected on the film, I was wondering whether all the reforms of *perestroika* in recent months would be a true awakening out of the long night of communism, or whether the "patient" would relapse. And somehow, our newfound ties with Erika made such reflection even more urgent. I wondered whether, after all her family had been through, a better life would ever become a realistic prospect for her.

By this time, Erika was taking advantage of the thaw in the government's attitude to the victims of the years of repression. They were now granting access to the former KGB files. The ongoing work of a new advocacy organization called "Memorial" [24] (pronounced Memoriale in Russian), was beginning to reveal more and more about the fate of Stalin's victims. Aleksandr Solzhenitsyn had recently returned to live in Russia again, after his exile first in Europe and then in America, a total of twenty years. Ironically, his popularity in the West never really translated into the role he had hoped for—a political savior of his people. Meanwhile, we continued to wait for more information concerning Jakob.

*Erika and Oleg's dacha outside Moscow*

Erika was beginning to feel sad at the prospect of our life close to her in Moscow coming to an end, since she deeply valued her sense that we were now "family." We spent more time with her and Oleg,

---

[24] See www.memo.ru for the Russian website and for an English version, see www.memo.ru/eng.

and with her son, Seryozha (Sergey), and his young family. Oleg was genuinely interested in discovering more about the faith of the Mennonites. He warmly welcomed our sharing of passages from the Bible, which he had never read. Oleg had worked for a government institute all his life, involved with rocket research. Erika told us he was the typical professor—brilliant at his work, but totally impractical when it came to any household repairs!

During the last months in Moscow, we spent some time with Erika at their family dacha on the outskirts of Moscow. They had been granted eligibility for this property because of Oleg's job at the government institute, which officially owned the piece of land. Other employees there had also constructed simple, country cabins on the small plots allocated to them in the quiet forested area. There they were free to enjoy the fresh air and nature, growing a few vegetables of their own. These *ogorods* (vegetable gardens) were a lifeline for many during the hard economic times they were facing.

*Herb, Erika, and Maureen with Erika's granddaughter at Erika and Oleg's dacha*

It was touching to see how much pleasure Erika derived from her simple existence there, taking us for walks in the nearby woods where she would pick all sorts of herbs, wild berries, or mushrooms. It gave her a sense of freedom that she did not feel in her apartment in Moscow. She enjoyed the fruit and vegetables from her little plot, making preserves and jams. She was a true Russian like our mother Mary in this respect, enjoying her woodstove and outhouse as a matter of course!

As we said goodbye to Erika, we knew that there were further chapters to our journey of discovery yet to unfold. We were grateful that the correspondence could continue.

## Erika's Visit to Canada

After we returned to Canada in 1995, our bonds with Erika were strengthened with her visit to our home in British Columbia. It was good to be able to host her and interpret Canada for her. She was happy to reacquaint herself with her newfound brother and to visit so many members of his extended family. She was impressed with the spaciousness of the Canadian homes, with the exception of our home—Mary's old "glasshouse"—which she said was "more like a Russian dacha."

She found visits to Mennonite churches somewhat overwhelming. The brightness and plainness of their architecture puzzled her; she assumed that churches, as in Russia, should be places of ornate decoration with icons and candles. Once in Moscow, when we had taken her to a Baptist Church, she had found it far too loud and bright—she missed the soft glow of candles and the smell of incense. She had whispered to me, "Maureen, this isn't a real church, is it?"

Coming into a Mennonite community in Canada, the daughter of a Jakob Reimer, whose roots were in the Mennonite settlements of Russia, it seemed ironic that her concept of Christianity was now irrevocably tied to the images of the Orthodox Church of Russia from which her ancestors had so vigorously separated themselves. Visiting the churches of her father's faith community with us, she showed interest and respect. But it would be to the state church of Russia that Erika would eventually turn in her later years. The great gulf fixed by Stalin's purges proved to be too great to bridge.

For Erika, a trained geologist, Canada was a fascinating place more for its flora and fauna, mountains and rocks, birds and trees. She eagerly studied these each day of her visit. It was clear here, too, that something in the common gene pool of the Reimer family enabled Erika and Harold to share many common interests. She had studied geology at Moscow University; and he shared her interest in gathering rocks. She was able to take back to Moscow only very few of those she collected during the weeks of her stay in Canada.

During Erika's visit we continued our discussions about Mary and Jakob's life. Perhaps it was at this time that she began to sense the crucial role Mary's second marriage had played in the lives of so many of the people she met in the Mennonite community. She became more and more interested in the C.F. Klassen story as she met many people who had been helped by him.

*Harold and Erika in British Columbia, 1995*

She was able to meet one elderly lady, Susie, who had been a neighbor of the Reimers in Karassan. From Susie she learned more about the lavish flower gardens her grandmother grew. She was impressed by the amount of information available about her father's home community in Crimea. At that time, we never dreamed that we would be able to make a pilgrimage there with Erika in 2001.

Erika was also impressed with the size of our families. In the Russia she knew, very few people had more than one child. Indeed, given their cramped housing, larger families were a virtual impossibility. She enjoyed getting to know all our children and grandchildren. I recall how impressed people had been in Moscow when I told them how many grandchildren I had. They would always sigh and say, *"Bagati, bagati"* (rich, rich!). Russians love children and greatly value family. Communism seemed to have robbed them of a full enjoyment of that blessing.

We spent one lovely weekend as an extended family in the beautiful home of our cousins Diet (Dietrich) and Lenora Kroeker on Pender Island, just off the coast of British Columbia. Many happy times were shared around the table, overlooking the ocean, watching the beautiful sunsets, and chatting with Harold and Ruthie, Wally (Walfried) and Helene, and the Kroekers. Erika loved the ocean-side setting; she spent hours walking the beaches and gathering interesting rocks for her collection (most of which she had to leave behind in Canada with me). She treasured times sitting on a swing beside the ocean with her brother, Harold. It saddened her to think that their friendship had so short a duration, knowing that his cancer was progressing. She had brought him a popular herbal remedy from Russia to drink daily, hoping in vain to halt the progress of the disease. Harold hated the taste, but drank it in part out of loyalty to Erika's good intentions.

When it came time for Erika to go home to Russia, the parting with Harold was a difficult one. We all knew that his life was ebbing away and that the brother and sister would not meet again. For Harold, the discovery of his mother's first marriage, the identity of his father, and this newfound sister, represented a somewhat overwhelming epilogue to a full and happy life in Canada. For Erika, these discoveries were bittersweet as there was still much that remained a mystery to her about her father's life and death.

Harold's health declined that autumn, but he did manage to be present at one last family Christmas. As one who had helped many people with their income tax returns, he was determined to live into the new tax year of 1996. Perhaps he shared that streak of determination so evident in Erika's persistent search for him. He died on the first day of January in 1996.

We had the sad task of calling Erika in Moscow to tell her the news. She accepted it with her typical stoicism, borne of the many years that she had lived under communism.

I was grateful to learn later in a letter from Erika that she had then visited the church of St. Cosmos and St. Damian. There she bought a small icon of Jesus that she treasured.

After Harold's death, there would be further discoveries that would bring her closer to learning the circumstances of her father's death and the location of his final resting place. And questions about Mary would continue to occupy her thoughts. Erika always regretted that she was unable to complete her ongoing search while Harold was still alive.

So it was that after we had been in Canada for a few years, we got news that Erika's persistent inquiries about her father's life and death had at last borne fruit.

# 10

# A KGB Revelation in Moscow

The long-awaited letter from Erika with more details of her father's fate finally arrived in the year 2000 when we had been back in Canada for several years. We were grateful that at last all her perseverance was being rewarded.

This much we already knew: sometime after Erika's birth in Bukhara, Uzbekistan, the family moved back to the Moscow region, where Jakob worked as an engineer in several different factories and energy facilities, and for a time in the music recording company Aprilevka. Then, in the fateful year 1937, with thousands of other Soviet citizens, Jakob was arrested abruptly from his home in Moscow and never seen again by his wife, Vera, or his daughter, Erika. Information about his ultimate fate had been left dangling for many years.

The Stalinist campaign of "dekulakization" (1929–1932) had largely succeeded in ridding the new Soviet society of counter-revolutionaries, capitalists, bourgeoisie, landowners, intellectuals, clerics, and all those perceived to be enemies of the Revolution (i.e., *kulaks*, literally, "hard fisted ones"). Anne Konrad's own search for her lost and disappeared relatives, narrated in *Red Quarter Moon*, characterizes the assertions being made during this brutal period as follows: "Propagandists shouted that 'land-grabbing, bloodsucker' bosses had abused and exploited workers for centuries for personal gain and these enemies should be removed ruthlessly."[25]

Jakob's arrest in 1937 was part of what became known as the "Great Terror" (1936–1938), another Stalinist purge. This time the purge was aimed at removing all those perceived to be a threat to national security. After his arrest, Erika and Vera lived for years without

---

[25] Konrad, *Red Quarter Moon*, 39.

any information about Jakob or what had happened to him. There was only silence.

Finally, after years of silence, Vera and Erika did get some information about Jakob in 1957 when his case was reviewed. Vera had written a complaint to the Military Prosecutor of the USSR, requesting an appeal in the case of her husband, Jakob J. Reimer. This led to a review of his case and the acknowledgment that he had been wrongfully convicted. His rehabilitation—apparently a common practice at the time—was an attempt by the regime to recognize its mistakes and false convictions.

Erika once related this to us with grim ironic humor, telling us of the rehabilitation letter she got from the authorities. They regretted the fate of her father and told her that she could now travel free on the Metro! She was also awarded a modest sum of money from the government as compensation for his lost wages. With this money she bought a carpet that hangs in good Russian style on a wall in her home.

Erika had never, however, been given access to the court documents with the transcripts of his actual trial in 1937.

In the late 1990s, after long years of silence, Russian people were at last getting a glimpse into the final months of their loved ones' lives. It was at that time, after the breakup of the Soviet Union, that relatives of those who died during Stalin's repression, with the help of advocacy organizations like "Memorial," were given access to the KGB files. Since our return to Canada, we continued to get letters from Erika, updating us on the progress of her search for details about her father's trial and his death.

Finally, in the year 2000, after repeated visits to the KGB bureaucratic offices and archives, she obtained the prison photograph of her father at the time of his arrest; and most importantly, she was given access to the official transcript of his interrogation. She laboriously copied in longhand all this information, sending it to us in her typical, closely handwritten writing on twelve small pages.[26]

Herb and I carefully translated the interrogation transcript and were greatly surprised by what we found. From the "jaws of the lion," as it were, we learned details about Jakob and Mary, and their relationship to CF and others. We learned details that we would otherwise never have known. In our view, this knowledge helped bring us one step closer to dispelling the unfounded allegations implicating

---

[26] A copy of Erika's letter, dated December 12, 2000, along with the transcription of the KGB interrogation and our translation is included in the the Mary Brieger Klassen personal papers collection, Centre for Mennonite Brethren Studies, Winnipeg.

CF in the failure of Mary's marriage to Jakob. It also answered questions that had remained unanswered for years concerning Jakob's relationship with CF, including the depth of their friendship and trust.

The photograph that Erika sent us of her father was particularly poignant. It shows Jakob in prison with a lean haggard face and a torn scarf around his neck. His cheeks are hollow and his brow is deeply lined. It was a far cry from the picture in Erika's album—the one showing a handsome young lover, standing tall beside his young bride. This photograph was very precious to Erika. It is the last image she had of her father. She took great pride in sending it to us in Canada.

*Jakob Reimer, prison photograph, 1937*

All these many years later, we try to understand the meaning of the interrogation process recorded in her letter. What did they want to accomplish by it? The KGB archives report that in 1937, there were 1,196,369 prisoners sentenced for "counter-revolutionary crimes." In the Moscow *oblast* (region) alone, during the years of the "Great Terror," thousands of these prisoners were executed and many more were sent into exile. What determined Jakob's sentence? And what was his crime? Was it his simple confession that he corresponded with C.F. Klassen, now a foreigner and the guardian of his son Harold?

## The Trial of Jakob J. Reimer

We try to imagine the setting of these statements on the pages Erika sent us. We can visualize him as he is brought before his interrogators, wary but determined. This is the exchange recorded in the transcript.

*Q.1. Why didn't you serve in the Red Army?*
*A.1. I didn't want to fight.*

Jakob was alluding to his Mennonite position on non-violence. We know that he served officially in an Ambulance Unit, an alternative way provided by the government to serve his country during time of war.

*Q.2. Do you have any relatives abroad?*
*A.2. My first wife, Mary Klassen, left Russia with her husband, Cornelius Klassen, and my son, who is now fourteen. They went to Canada in 1928, settling in Winnipeg.*

*Q.3. Who is Klassen and how long have you known him?*
*A.3. I have known him from school days in Karassan. He was a friend of my brother, Ivan. He was also a German-speaking colonist.*

Then follows the most interesting part of the transcript; it contains facts about his continuing relationship with CF, which neither we nor Erika knew clearly before.

*Q.4. It is known to this investigation that you met Klassen again in Moscow. Did you correspond with him after he emigrated to Canada? Tell us about this.*
*A.4. Yes, I met with him in Moscow. C.F. Klassen was a good friend and a frequent visitor in our home there. He worked for a Mennonite relief agency that delivered famine relief. My wife, Mary Brieger, and I were divorced in 1925. After that, she married C.F. Klassen. Klassen and I remained good friends before his departure. After he left for Canada, I continued to write to him in the German language.*

It is our regret that none of those letters have come down to us. Perhaps CF's letters in reply contained friendly reporting of the new life in Canada and the life of the young son, now in the custody of his old friend there.

The next question takes a more serious accusatory tone.

*Q.5. It is known to this investigation that Klassen demanded sabotage work from you and that you sent him secret espionage information.*
*A.5. As you know, Klassen was a secretary and member of the executive of the All-Russian Mennonite Agricultural Union. In Canada, he also worked on behalf of the Mennonites. All he asked of me was how the German-speaking Mennonites were doing in the USSR and in Moscow. He did not demand any sabotage work of me. I sent him Russian postage stamps for his collection. The*

*correspondence with Mary had to do with family matters. My son, who is now fourteen, lives with them.*

It is touching that Jakob refers to one of CF's favorite hobbies, his stamp collection, which he maintained for years in Canada. A further line of questioning is then taken up, relating to Jakob's musical activities.

*Q.6. Do you know about the organization "Crescendo"? What kind of organization was it and what was your relationship with it?*

*A.6. Yes, I know it. It is a society of music lovers. They played symphonic music. There were Germans and Russians among them. Someone from the conservatory led the orchestra. I also went to their concerts.*

They continue to pursue the German connection.

*Q.7. Which other Germans did you know and have in your home?*

*A.7. Franz Wall was manager of the hospital in Muntau in the Melitopol region. I knew him from the time of my childhood. The last time he was in our home was 1936. He was arrested in 1936 and exiled to Siberia.*

*Peter Froese was the director of the All-Russian Mennonite Agricultural Union. He was arrested in 1931* [Peter Froese was actually arrested in Moscow on October 15, 1929].

*Garri Helms was a former director of the Church Council of the Lutheran Church. He is a dentist and helped me with my teeth.*

*Rudolf Claassen was a doctor who lived in Moscow and then left for Canada in 1927* [Rudolf Claassen actually left Moscow in 1925[27]].

*Abram Reimer lived in Moscow and worked as a driver for the Central executive committee.*

*Isaac Thiessen was a German Mennonite. He was the head doctor at Kichkas hospital. He was arrested and exiled. But I didn't know him. He was a friend of my brother, Ivan, but I haven't seen him since 1932.*

It is clear from this line of questioning—establishing Jakob's connections with foreigners—that they were trying to construct a case of espionage and treason against Reimer, a case that would give them cause to condemn him to the firing squad.

Jakob was one of many who were being convicted of treasonous liaisons with German-speaking people who had departed the Soviet Union many years before. Such convictions were a pretense, contrived in order to sentence thousands to death—an ethnic cleansing strategy that ended up purging the nation of many of its most gifted and upstanding citizens. The nation was hemorrhaging its choicest sons.

---

[27] Rudolf Abram Claassen and his wife Selma left Moscow on September 20, 1925, arriving in Montreal on October 9, 1925, and settling in Winnipeg. Canadian Mennonite Board of Colonization card number 1980.

It is touching to realize that in 1937 Jakob could still give the exact age of his son.

Peter Froese was, of course, a close friend of the Mennonite group in Moscow. In 1937, Froese was still in the Yaroslavl prison just outside Moscow after his arrest in 1929. Froese was also a close friend of CF's in Moscow, working with him in the AMLV Agricultural Union.

One other name mentioned is Rudolf Claassen, who had already immigrated to Canada. He became a pioneer physician at the Concordia Hospital in Winnipeg. It is interesting to learn that Jakob and Rudolf were good friends. This mention in Jakob's trial transcript was the first time we had heard this. Doctor Rudolf A. Claassen was a very good friend to the Klassen family during the Winnipeg years. He always supported Mary kindly through various health crises, especially when she was left alone with her family while CF was gone on his travels.

Jakob had furnished the KGB with the required names, but every one of them was now safely away from incrimination. He had also, so many years later, provided us with a clearer picture of his circle in Moscow during those turbulent years of the 1920s.

*Q.8. Did you know a man named Lustvig?*

*A.8. Yes, I did. He came to Aprilevka to find a job in 1936. But he didn't find one. There was no vacancy.*

Aprilevka was the record company Jakob later worked for in Moscow. Then the questioning returns to the theme of Jakob's music.

*Q.9. How often in the circle of friends did you play fascist anthems on the piano?*

*A.9. I never played fascist anthems. I only played English and German hymns.*

The line of questioning seems so benign, hardly enough to base a conviction worthy of the death sentence. How could singing the beautiful Mennonite hymns of his youth be construed as treasonous?

Apparently, corresponding with capitalist enemies had become a Soviet crime after the rise of Hitler in Germany. The Soviets were likely frantic about Hitler's anti-Bolshevism and thus targeted German speakers in the USSR as traitors and saboteurs. They probably feared that should there be a war, these ethnic minorities within the USSR would assist Germany. The German-speaking Russians were no doubt already spying for the enemy, or so they thought.

And so it was that Jakob Reimer, the accused traitor, was actually sentenced to death for his relationship with several German-speaking Mennonites, including the man who was taking care of Mary and his son.

At this point in her letter, Erika commented, "Papa always denied that he was a traitor working on behalf of the German intelligence service and their embassy." Surprisingly, Jakob's denial of any wrongdoing or espionage was retained in the interrogation transcript.

Then she added some further information. On December 27, 1937, two days before her father was shot, Erika's mother, Vera, had been summoned and interrogated. She had been asked about which Germans had visited their home. She had repeated the names of those already given by Jakob, adding one name, Cornelius Fast.

The transcript then records the interrogation of some of Jakob's co-workers from the factory where he had worked under the auspices of the NKVD. They were brought in to testify against him. Their names were Jakob Nemchinski, Mikhail Ryabov, and Timofei Nozhkin. Nemchinski was a Pole with a good education, who had worked previously for the People's Commissariat of Internal Affairs (NKVD). Each of them is recorded as giving negative testimony concerning Jakob's work.

Ryabov testified:

*He did bad technical work causing damage to the equipment. He made the engines overwork, causing them to break down frequently. He paid the workers wrong salaries. He was a very suspicious person. He was the cause of the breakdown of twenty engines. He had a negative attitude to the government and made counter-revolutionary speeches.*

Nemchinski repeated the same accusations:

*Reimer was an anti-Soviet person, a saboteur. His attitude to equipment was criminal. That's why there were so many fires. Reimer hindered the building of the power station. He caused the breakdown of all the electrical equipment and created a fire hazard.*

This is followed by the "Indictment of the Prisoner":

*Based on this testimony we have reached the following conclusions concerning the accused prisoner No. 6596 J.J. Reimer.*

*On the basis of our investigation, we conclude that the actions of J.J. Reimer, a German-Mennonite, prove him guilty of the activity of espionage, through his contacts with other German-Mennonites: Helms, Thiessen, and Wall. He maintained regular contact with C.F. Klassen, a German-Mennonite in Canada, passing on to him information about the situation of German-Mennonites in the USSR.*

*In the time of the Great Citizens' War, he was found to be in Crimea serving with Wrangel's White Army.*

*Being a counter-revolutionary person, he worked against the Soviet authorities.*

*According to the testimony of Ryabov and Nemchinski, Reimer, an engineer, was a saboteur at the Aprilevka record factory. By deliberately running down the electric network, he caused the destruction of more than twenty motors from 1934–1936, resulting in many systematic breakdowns at the factory.*

Then Jakob was asked:

*Q.10. Do you confess that you are guilty of the declared accusations?*

*A.10. I deny any connection with the workers at the German embassy and deny any spy activity on the territory of the USSR, and deny any sabotage activity. I am not guilty.*

*(signature) J. Reimer*

*Transcript No. 106: Decision of the NKVD on December 23, 1937. J.J. Reimer is guilty and to be shot to death.*
*Sentence was carried out on December 29, 1937.*

## Trial Review

Erika's letter went on to describe a dramatic postscript to the trial documentation—Jakob's KGB file also included testimony from the trial review completed twenty years later.

In 1957, Erika's mother had requested an inquiry into Jakob's case. The inquiry was granted and two of the three witnesses who had incriminated Jakob were called. Nemchinski admitted to giving false information, only saying what he was asked to say. He had signed the incriminating document without even reading it! He went on to testify that Jakob was an excellent engineer and did only first-rate, sacrificial service at the factory where they had worked together. Now he could only say good things about his colleague:

*I now believe my testimony about Reimer was wrong. I can explain my testimony by the fact that in 1937 any sorts of problems of any employee were regarded as sabotage.*

The other co-worker, Nozhkin, went even further when asked what kind of person Jakob was.

*He was my boss. I can only say good things about him. He was a good engineer. He put a lot of time into production; every effort was made to make the plant work better. Factory workers respected and valued Reimer's attitude to work and for the assistance he gave them. No one from the electrical department could say anything negative about him. I never saw him in any hostile action. I remember Reimer as a decent honest man. After his arrest, I was questioned and I said the same things that I am saying now.*

When Nozhkin was presented with the record from 1937, he added, "I declare that these statements are untrue. I could not have given that testimony." He then continued to paint a very positive picture of Jakob. Concerning the way he supervised the work of the factory, he said:

*We always had accidents at the plant and still have. The plant has operated since 1905 and the electrical equipment is old. Reimer, as chief of the electrical department, did everything to lower the number of accidents. He took care of production and was doing everything to avoid accidents. He did everything to improve production. In 1937, I signed the transcript without even reading it.*

At this point in her copying of the trial transcript, Erika added the following sentences in parentheses, noting the overwhelming fear that affected everyone in those years.

*In 1937, when a young man was called to the KGB, I think his knees were trembling with fear that he would not be released. He would be glad to do whatever was needed to get out of there as soon as possible.*

The evidence of redaction in the transcript to ensure a guilty verdict was clear. But how much redaction? Some aspects of Jakob's voice and character seemed to be discernible, in spite of the propaganda machinery. However, we will likely never know the complete answer to these questions with absolute certainty.

Erika did not tell us what comfort Vera received from the new assessment of her husband's life. Hopefully, she took some consolation from the valuations given in a more sober moment, when his good qualities could again be commended. But for Erika, the irony was bittersweet, and too late to be of any consequence. On the basis of this new testimony, the family received the exoneration of their father, as many in those years did, at the hands of a regime anxious to wipe the blood of millions from their hands.

While aspects of the official trial transcript remain suspect, it did establish two realities for us. First, it was clear that Jakob's connections with his own people, German-speaking people, including C.F. Klassen, proved to be his downfall and led to his death sentence. Second, the Soviet system was able to obtain a conviction on the basis of any trumped-up charge it chose.[28] In Jakob's case, this involved false

---

[28] See Anne Konrad's similar account of reading KGB transcripts in 2007 of the interrogation of two of her uncles (Konrad, *Red Quarter Moon*, 288–302). "The interrogation files showed only how the Soviet system worked. Torture can get most people to confess to false charges. And the complicit interrogators? So often these agents later experienced the same fate as their victims. What a waste. Wasted lives" (302).

information about his professional work as an engineer. The loss of her father for such twofold duplicity was the tragedy Erika spent a lifetime seeking to redress.

For us, however, the significant fact was that after years of being unable to answer satisfactorily Erika's questions about her father's relationship with C.F. Klassen, we finally had Jakob's own answers, in his own words. We heard his voice above the noise of misinformation, and we received it from the actual KGB files, the organ of his destruction. The reference to CF's stamp collection, along with Jakob's concern for his son and his recollection of Harold's age, could hardly have been concocted by interrogators. We could now say without doubt: Jakob and CF were friends and remained so until Jakob's untimely death.

It now remained for Erika to see if her father's final resting place could ever be determined, given the large numbers who passed out of the infamous Lubyanka prison every night, a number that reached its peak in that worst of all years, 1937.

That revelation was to come in a year or two, testing the patience of this daughter who, it seemed, had waited a lifetime to pull together the threads of her father's tragic life. She had labored long to bring all this information to the light. She closed her long twelve-page letter with these words.

*I am glad I can send you the picture of Papa in prison. As fate would have it, he has more relatives in Canada now than in Russia. For their sake I did this research. And of course, I did it for myself. It is a pity Harold did not have the chance to learn these details about his father's life.*

# 11

# To Ukraine in 2001

It was hard for Erika, so late in her life, at age seventy-four, to receive details about the final crisis of her father's life. All that remained now was to discover his final resting place, and she continued to search for that information.

As she looked back over her life, Erika recalled that there was never a time when her mother lost her fear of the cruel regime that had torn her husband from her. Jakob's siblings were all arrested at some time during the years of the repression. After Vera's terrifying summons to the KGB two days before Jakob was shot, Erika's mother always feared that the fateful knock would come on her door one night to arrest her and separate her from her child forever.

Children whose parents were both imprisoned became wards of the state and stigmatized for life. Many were placed in orphanages that had a terrible reputation for neglect and poor care. Others became *besprizorniki*, literally, "those without protection," as I described earlier. Practically speaking, they were roving beggars with no fixed abode. They often terrorized whole communities, begging or stealing to survive. Gratefully, Erika was spared that fate.

After Jakob's death, Erika's mother eventually remarried, taking her new husband's name, Krasnohorskaya. At that time, as a protection against any further persecution for her association with the German name Reimer, Erika took the name Krasnohorskaya, too. It was under that name that she applied to Moscow University and studied in the geology faculty.

The advocacy group "Memorial," formed during the *perestroika* years, had been especially helpful to Erika in gaining access to the KGB files revealing the details of her father's death. But she longed to know a place where she could lay flowers on his grave, a ritual considered very important to Russian people. "Memorial" would eventually help her do even this, giving her the final chapter of closure concerning her father.

Erika, however, realized that before making the pilgrimage to his final resting place, there was another pilgrimage she wished to make. She had never visited the place of her father's origin, the Mennonite village of Karassan in Crimea where Jakob Reimer was born. So it was that in the summer of 2001, we were able to help her fulfill this desire.

## The Mennonite Centre of Ukraine

In the year 2001, Herb and I received a unique invitation through Herb's old friend, Prof. Harvey Dyck from the University of Toronto. We were asked to come back to the former Soviet Union and take a short assignment in Ukraine for four months, helping with a new venture there.

In order to respond to the invitation, we needed to obtain a leave of absence from the ministry we were then doing for Logos Canada. After our return to Canada, this was the Christian mission we had begun to work for, supporting new missionaries in the former Soviet Union. We were glad to utilize our Russian language skills, translating their missionary letters for the Mennonite people in Canada, who were eager to support an ongoing work of evangelism in their former homeland. Logos granted us a leave of absence for four months, and we flew to Zaporozhye, Ukraine.

Our task was to pioneer yet another Mennonite Centre! This time it was to be located in the heart of the former Molochna Mennonite colony, in Molochansk, formerly known as Halbstadt. Professor Harvey Dyck had gathered a group from Toronto, Canada, called Friends of the Mennonite Centre of Ukraine (FOMCU), to sponsor the project. Our assignment as first directors of the work involved overseeing the renovation of a former *Mädchenschule* (Girls' high school) that was to become the new Centre.

The small school, set in a quiet lot on a side street, was built by the Mennonites of Halbstadt in 1910 for the education of their girls. It was purchased back from the government by the Canadian group, who had the vision to restore the building and use it as a base to bring humanitarian aid to the Ukrainian people now living on the lands once occupied by the prosperous Mennonites. Our short stay there saw the beginnings of the transformation of the building from beneath its many layers of Soviet white paint, to become more like the little red-brick school house of the bygone era.

*Mennonite Centre in Molochansk, Ukraine*

In ensuing years, the activities conducted in the Centre would make a significant contribution to the well-being of countless Ukrainians on the soil of those original Mennonite colonies and estates. Some of the volunteers, who followed us for short periods of service, contributed their considerable musical gifts to the great enrichment of the local population. Many medical clinics were conducted. The substantial humanitarian help also included activities for children and regular social gatherings for the many senior citizens facing economic hardship.

It was an enriching experience to live for a short time at the place where the life of the Russian Mennonites had begun. The old life of the town was still perceptible, with its broad streets and solid buildings, though the ravages of time and civil war had stripped them of their former glory. But when spring burst in on us, with all the blossoming trees and colorful red tulips, I couldn't help but reflect that nature defies the march of politics and history, renewing the earth year by year from seeds that may have been planted in a happier time decades earlier.

In the course of our work, we traveled to many of the former Mennonite villages, seeking to bring some material and spiritual aid to this now economically depressed region. It was poignant to see the occasional Mennonite solid brick house that had survived the ravages of civil war and communism. We noticed that many of the fine institutional buildings like schools and hospitals had been preserved and were still being used.

One impressive example stands on the main street of Molochansk. It is the former prestigious Halbstadt *Zentralschule* (high school), with its impressive Doric-style columns fronting the street. The building is proudly used as a municipal center today. The Muntau hospital still stands at the edge of the town. FOMCU was able to help the hospital by providing additional medical equipment. That such structures remain intact is evidence of their enduring quality and ongoing potential to contribute to the recovery of life and culture after years of devastation. Hospitals and nursing schools are a tribute to the merciful lifestyle of the long-lost presence of the Mennonites in Russia.

## Erika's Visit to Karassan

Towards the end of our time in Molochansk, Erika asked if she might come and pay us a brief visit. It might well be the last time we would see her. She could only leave her husband—now suffering from severe Alzheimer's disease—for a brief few days. We consented and Erika arrived at the train station in Melitopol a few days later. She had aged since our last meeting and was clearly greatly stressed from her unrelieved care of her husband, Oleg. We hoped the break would be pleasant for her. She commented that it was nice to be around "normal" people for a while!

During our time together, our conversation repeatedly returned to the topic of the letter she had recently sent us in Canada containing her copied record of the trial of her father, Jakob Reimer. She said, "I never realized my father and your father, C.F. Klassen, were such good friends."

She wanted to go over again the many pages she had copied from the transcript to be sure that we had translated the information correctly. She had spent a lifetime searching for the truth about her family, her long-lost brother, and her father's fate. She wanted to be sure that accurate information would reach those who should know about it in the West.

One of the main purposes of her visit was to travel together with us to Karassan, the birth place of her father. It was a cool, cloudy day as we took the road past the familiar villages, past Melitopol and beyond. It would be about a three-hour drive to Crimea. Erika was quiet and thoughtful on the way there, wondering what, if anything, would be left of her father's birthplace. Would she meet anyone in any way connected with the Reimer family? We wondered how much of the structure of this former thriving Mennonite village would have survived the ravages of time and history.

In our minds were images of the village we had seen in photo collections. I remembered one from the dedication of the school in 1905. It shows an impressive brick facade with lofty windows. Almost obscuring the tall iron railings—set between solid brick pillars of the front fence running the entire breadth of the building—is a huge gathered company of dark-clothed teachers, students, and other dignitaries. Would anything be left of that fine era?

We picnicked briefly along the way and arrived in the village of Karassan just after lunch. It now had a new Ukrainian name, Rivne (Rovnoe in Russian). All was quiet as if the noon-hour lull was extended into the early afternoon. We didn't see many people as we strolled around the deserted dusty streets. A scene of almost total deterioration greeted us. There was little evidence of the agricultural Eden that had attracted settlers so many years before.

*Karassan* Zentralschule *where C.F. Klassen studied with Jakob and Ivan Reimer*

From William Schroeder and Helmut Huebert's *Mennonite Historical Atlas*, we knew the layout of the village from the years when it had been a thriving Mennonite community, so it was not hard to locate the school that we were looking for. Renowned across the entire population of Mennonites in the colonies, it was here that Jakob Reimer and his brother, Ivan, had first met C.F. Klassen, who had boarded with his Aunt Greta in order to attend this reputable institute.

## To Ukraine in 2001

The shell of the fine old building was still discernible. Set back from the main road with what was once a kind of public square out front, it stood overgrown with tall grass. The stately architecture was now crumbling and the building, until fairly recently still used as a school, had fallen into disuse. No sign of its old life was now perceptible. Erika absorbed the sight reflectively, but soon wanted to seek other landmarks.

The house where her father was born was no longer standing. Old photographs show that, like all other Mennonite homes, it boasted a large garden and was bordered by some of the fragrant local trees like acacia or mulberry. Photographs in Erika's album show a time when Mary visited this place. She also lived here for a short time, as mentioned earlier, during the difficult early years of the Revolution and civil war. Mary and Jakob fled here to find a way to support themselves and be fed. Most Mennonites of Crimea grew their own grapes for domestic use since the climate was very favorable, but there was little sign of that now.

Passing down the old main street, the dwellings we saw seemed more recent; and speaking with the occasional passerby, we found this to be true. Most were of typical Soviet construction, poorly built with corrugated composite roofing. The inhabitants were totally ignorant of any former presence in the village or of its history. We saw a few ruins of former finer homes. The original church looked pathetically dilapidated, with the words *Klyb* (club) on the side indicating its use as a community center. There was evidence of extreme poverty everywhere. Erika sighed, "*Pechalny, pechalny*" (sad, sad). Only the leafy trees of the main street evoked an echo of scenes seen in the photographs in Erika's album.

When we reached the hospital, one of the few original Mennonite buildings, our spirits lifted to see bright flowers in a circular flowerbed in front of the door. Erika recalled her father's stories about the beautiful flowers his mother had grown in this village. The cheerful flowers brought to mind some of the ghosts of a Mennonite past. We thought of a time when the inhabitants of this place were known for their deeds of compassion and care for the needy, like war casualties.

At the local government office, we found one older woman who had heard mention of a Mennonite past, but no one recalled anyone of the name of Reimer. The cemetery had no memorial stone to Jakob's aged mother and survivor of the sad saga of her family's suffering. Erika told us that Jakob's mother had been sent back here just after her two daughters were exiled to Kazakhstan. She had died almost immediately.

A fine rain had now begun to fall. We had not experienced the usual warm welcome of the Crimean sun, and so we were ready to take shelter in the car for the drive back to Molochansk. There was not much conversation at first in the car, and Erika kept repeating the phrase, *"Pechalny, pechalny"* (sad, sad). There had been little here for her to link with her father's life. Even a brief survey of the local cemetery yielded no familiar names. However, she had made the pilgrimage and fulfilled her desire to see his birthplace. The rest of her quest would remain in her pensive meditations.

As the car neared the more familiar terrain of Ukraine again, Erika voiced another desire. Perhaps she was reflecting again on the strange connection of those of us in the car. Or maybe she was reaching for a gesture that would bind her to the memory of a woman who had once been loved by her father, the mother of the man driving our car, my husband. Or was she still searching for a way to celebrate the intertwining of our lives, even though those ties had been strained by painful events?

Karassan had yielded no opportunities to celebrate those ties. As we passed through a deserted former Mennonite village, Erika suddenly said, "I want to stop and buy something here, something to remember Mary."

I wasn't sure what she had in mind, and furthermore, the almost total absence of any stores in the place seemed to render the request impossible. But eventually we came across the only public building, a combination post office, store, and gas station.

On entering the store part, we looked in vain for saleable produce, even so much as a chocolate bar. A few items like cigarettes and some limp local vegetables were visible on a side table. Suddenly at the back, on a tall shelf, we saw some large jars containing rather odd items—candied fruit slices of orange and lemon. I cannot explain the very strange coincidence of their presence in this barren store. All I know is that I immediately recalled that Mary Klassen had always bought such a confectionary at Funk's Supermarket in Clearbrook. It was a Mennonite grocery store that served the immigrant community for many decades. She always had them in a particular glass dish, one that I have to this day. Mary would have them on her Christmas table when we visited her. It was the only thing we could buy in the store; it definitely was something that brought Mary vividly to our memory.

As we climbed back into the car and drove the rest of the way back to Molochansk—remembering Mary—it seemed that the sweetness in our mouths was compensating for the sadness in our hearts. And so we drove away from Karassan in silence, reflecting on the memories that were hidden there.

While Erika was still with us, at her request we visited some of the nearby former Mennonite villages, like Alexanderkrone and Lichtfelde. This was where C.F. Klassen's grandparents were from. She was interested again to see some of the old buildings, like the school and the church, which had withstood the devastations of time and history.

*Old windmill at Alexanderkrone, Ukraine, 2001*

It was particularly interesting to see the old windmill still standing; it had been in use until 1952. Such windmills had been common to the Mennonite way of life in the Danzig area of Prussia, before they immigrated to Russia. They had also once been numerous in their colonies in Ukraine, too. This is the last known Mennonite windmill in Russia. Standing serenely, surveying the peaceful rural scene on that sunny afternoon, we couldn't help imagining the former days of Mennonite village life, before the beautiful tapestry of peace and prosperity was forever torn apart.

One interesting feature was the old Mennonite church. With some renovations and a corrugated roof, it had become a Russian Orthodox Church. For Erika, the transition seemed quite logical. She appreciated the value of a truly Russian form of Christianity, and she was by now quite removed from her father's Mennonite perspective on Christian faith. But the church doors were locked; so we were unable to go inside.

## Saying Goodbye

Back in Molochansk, our four-month assignment was soon coming to an end. During the months at the Ukraine Mennonite Centre, we discovered almost no "trace" Mennonites. The only one we met was a widow, Olga Fast. Married to a Russian, she had been exiled to Siberia in the Stalin years because of her German connections.

When Olga returned to Molochansk after exile, she discovered that her husband had taken a succession of other wives. She declined his invitation to remarry and now she lived alone in a tiny shack on the outskirts of town. Almost blind, she relied on the help of the nearby church people to help her survive her meager existence. The church she attended was the beautifully renovated former Petershagen Mennonite Church in nearby Kutuzovka. Strong ties to the experiences of her youth had drawn her back to the faith after many years. Resuming her maiden name, she sent greetings to any in Canada who remembered her father, a teacher in Halbstadt's happier years.

We did, however, take part in one memorable event that goes to the heart of the Mennonite experience in Ukraine. During our last weeks, we attended the dedication of a memorial to those who died in the tragedy at Eichenfeld in 1919. At that fateful time, the notorious anarchist bandits, Makhnovtsy, attacked the village and killed eighty-two residents. This is twice as many who died in the infamous massacre at Glencoe, Scotland, something that is forever etched on the consciousness of British people.

*Olga Fast in Molochansk, Ukraine, 2001*

On May 27, 2001, eighty-two years later, a Mennonite tour group that included relatives of the deceased came to take part in the moving ceremony remembering the events of that night. Our friend, Prof. Harvey Dyck, was one of the organizers of the memorial and spoke at the commemoration.

Together in solemn pilgrimage, we walked across a field where some of the survivors had fled from the carnage of the massacre. Joining in the memorial were several local people who had no Mennonite connections, but were choosing to honor the past residents of their homeland.

In July 2001, we said goodbye to Erika for the last time and returned to British Columbia and our assignment with Logos. Erika's quest to locate the whereabouts of Jakob Reimer's grave had still not yielded any solid information, but she was not giving up and her persistence would eventually pay off once again. Still, the opportunity to hear and share stories during these four months helped us to interpret and find meaning in some of the saddest parts of our common pilgrimage.

# 12

# The End of the Road

From the first day that we had seen the photograph of Jakob and Mary in Erika's family album, it seemed that we had been slowly piecing together a picture of their lives. Yet we often had to wait patiently as the pieces came into view. The information, especially about Jakob, was not readily available, and only emerged over a period of several years. Erika was sad that her brother, Harold, had never learned the information she was now recovering about their father.

One year after our visit to Karassan with Erika, when we were in Canada, we received a letter from Erika along with a brochure of a place called the "Butovski Polygon: Russia's Golgotha."[29] The letter recounted her pilgrimage to this place on the outskirts of Moscow, and its significance for her father. It seems that she finally had been given information that Jakob Reimer's final resting place was, together with thousands of others, under the lush green grass of this peaceful place, a place that could not be more different than the quiet little village of his childhood.

The Russian authorities no longer made any secret of the millions who died under the Soviet regime. In fact, in a harsh stroke of ironic reality, they have detailed records to prove it. So when all the secrets of these years were opened up, people were able for the first time to ascertain where the remains of their relatives were buried. Of course, the nature of the mass killings and the mass graves themselves gave no opportunity for a personal memorial. Still, relatives made the most of the newly released information, taking pilgrimages to these places to bring some small closure to their years of nightmares, seeking after the truth that is the end of their tragic stories. It was all they could do.

---

[29] A copy of the Butovski Polygon brochure is included in the Mary Brieger Klassen personal papers collection, Centre for Mennonite Brethren Studies, Winnipeg.

*Butovski Polygon in Moscow, Russia's "Golgotha"*

So it was that Erika took this part of her pilgrimage alone, traveling from her home in the northern part of Moscow to this site located on the western fringe of the city. The Russian Orthodox Church has already taken ownership of the site and transformed it into a well-organized religious landmark. The glossy color brochure Erica sent us has pictures of ceremonies, shrines, and Russian icons.

From the brochure we learned that the Butovski Polygon is only one of hundreds of such burial sites on the soil of Russia. The first liturgy remembering the thousands who are buried here was celebrated in June 1995, just before we left Russia. At that time, we had no idea it held any special significance for our family.

The brochure stated that the Butovski Polygon was once a rifle shooting range situated on an old Russian estate named Drogino, famous since the sixteenth century. In the 1920s, it became an artillery range for the Soviet secret police. The surrounding villages became accustomed to the sounds of rifle shots there. But starting in 1937, the worst years of the Repression, the shots took on a more sinister character as surrounding inhabitants heard shots ringing out both day and night for months—if not years—on end.

When all the shooting was finished, the number of people buried in the network of mass graves was estimated to be close to 100,000. The names and details of 20,765 shot between August 1937 and October 1938 are recorded and now serve as a memorial to all who perished and are buried there, although Jakob Reimer's name is not one of those named in the record.

Among those recorded by the authorities are people from many nationalities; 60–70% were Russians, followed by Poles, Jews, Ukrainians, Germans, and Belo-Russians. Many were simple peasants and workers, but there were many from various Soviet departments as well. Also sharing this mass grave were citizens of some distinction—eminent scientists, engineers, military personnel, artists, writers, and other prominent individuals.

The pamphlet also contained a long list of well-known Russian Orthodox bishops and priests. Leaders from other faiths were also acknowledged, including three mullahs, a rabbi, and many Protestants and Catholics. All shared the same fate. Their lives crossed the path of the Revolution; they were perceived—in most cases irrationally—as a threat. The nightly journey to this infamous place of death during those years linked them together. Now they shared a common resting place.

In a quiet grove to one side of the memorial site there is a single wooden cross with a simple plaque leaning at its foot and a few flowers around it. This is the memorial to the countless *unnamed* victims who shared the same fate as the thousands of others in this horrendous place of nightly shootings. It is a quiet place, just a simple meadow with a few fruit trees. One laden apple tree stands to the left, with smaller trees spaced around. It is a place that lends itself to quiet reflection.

While at the memorial, Erika met a woman who shared more information about the daily slaughter that took place. Always eager for hard facts, Erika recounted in the letter to us that conversation with the woman whose father was also buried there.

*The woman knew one fellow who worked there when he was young and witnessed it all. He said that with bulldozers they dug deep ditches 500 meters long. The men who were to be shot were lined up on the edge of these ditches, facing the ditch. They shot them in the back of the head. All this misery this fellow witnessed. They fell into the ditch and their bodies were then riddled with rifle shots.*

A small Russian Orthodox Church at the site is dedicated to all these martyrs. The brochure concluded with the words, "Our confession and our hope is that neither persecution, nor death, nor any other thing can separate us from the love of God."

*Russian Orthodox Church at the Butovski Polygon in Moscow*

The facts must have been very hard for Erika to absorb as she stood there alone. The group shot that night on December 27, 1937, was simply added to the thousands who would meet their fate in the same brutal way. And yet Erika was grateful; finally, she was granted the opportunity to pay her last respects to the man whom she so fleetingly knew as her father, one who had left her with so many unanswered questions.

For the many thousands of people just like Vera and Erika, the disruption of family and the loss of close relatives was a common experience during those years. All three of Jakob's siblings died as a result of their experiences during the Repression years. In fact, her Aunt Sonja had been so changed by her prison years that Erika hardly recognized her when she met her on the day of her release. She had passed the figure of an old woman on the road, when suddenly it dawned on her that it was her aunt; hurriedly she turned around to embrace her. Katja and Ivan had also died many years ago. So on that day, Erika stood alone—the only offspring able to make the pilgrimage to their father's resting place.

Somehow, this elaborate and ornate memorial seemed utterly remote from the life she had known to be her father's. Now as she stood in the Butovski Polygon, she would have to summon her own ideas of what constituted a fitting memorial to her father.

Perhaps the plaintive Lermontov melody—the one I remember Mary singing—might have brought some comfort, if Erika recalled her father's voice singing the well-known song, with Lermontov's poetry expressing his own convictions.

*Forth I go,*
*Alone now on the highway,*
*Stony footfall leads me through the gloom,*
*Nightly stillness hearkens to the voice of God;*
*Silent stars are calling each to each.*

*Solemn stillness rules now the nightly scene;*
*All creation sleeps in night's blue depths.*
*Why then do I feel this pain within my heart?*
*What awaits me heavy on my breast?*

*Nothing further from this life do I desire,*
*No regrets I harbor from the past.*
*Perfect peace and freedom are my one desire,*
*When I take my final farewell breath.*

*Not for me the silence of death's slumber cold.*
*I would seek a living lasting rest.*
*So that life would still endure within my heart,*
*And forever live within this breast.*

—Lermontov (my translation)

And yet, I can't help wondering whether the last months of Jakob's life had given him opportunity to reflect more deeply on his life and the turn of events that brought him to this sad place.

Whatever distancing occurred during his later years, there was a period in his life when he happily accompanied the singing of joyful *Kernlieder* (core songs) from the Mennonite colonies. And according to the records of his KGB interrogation, he did play German hymns.

At his final moment, faced with the stark horror of the firing squad, Jakob may have chosen the words of one of the hymns of his youth.

*So nimm denn meine Hände, und führe mich*
*Bis an mein selig Ende und ewiglich!*
*Ich kann allein nicht gehen, nicht einen Schritt;*
*Wo Du wirst geh'n und stehen, da nimm mich mit.*

(Take Thou my hand, O Father, and lead Thou me
Until my journey endeth, eternally!
Alone I will not wander one single day;
Be Thou my true companion and with me stay.)

For Erika, this quiet rural scene marked the end of her road of discovery. But standing there on that quiet day did not fully lay to rest questions that still persisted in her heart about those hidden, turbulent years in Moscow that had marked the parting of the ways for so many people.

Anna Akhmatova, one of Russia's greatest poets, included Jakob and all his kin in her famous poem, *Requiem*, written about this terrible time. She was one who, instead of fleeing, chose to remain in Russia to share in the suffering of countless millions of her people.

*No foreign sky protected me,*
*No stranger's wing shielded my face,*
*I stand as witness to the common lot,*
*Survivor of that time, that place.*

In October 2012—ten years after the Butovski Polygon brought closure to Erika's pilgrimage of discovery—Herb and I received a sad email from Erika's son, Sergey. He informed us that his mother had died on October 1, 2012, at the age of eighty-six. Erika had been hospitalized because she was having difficulty breathing. It was discovered that she was suffering from colon cancer. Eventually, the cancer spread to her lungs. Sergey's email conveyed heartfelt greetings to all of Erika's "family in Canada." He wrote:

*My mother's recollections of her trip to Canada and the memories of all the relatives there were the best part of the last years of her life. She talked for hours about you all, your children and grandchildren. She loved you all so much.*

# 13

# Life After Moscow

What had become of the young Klassen family that sailed away to Canada in 1928, just at the height of the most troublesome years of the growing communist horror in their former homeland? And how does an immigrant community put behind them years of struggle and carve out a new existence, knowing that many of their kin remain in the land they have left?

The Klassens' departure had indeed been timely, for few Russian Mennonites managed the exodus to Canada after the Klassens left Moscow. Indeed, shortly after they left, their dear friend Peter Froese was arrested and spent the next ten years in prison. Had it been easy for them to turn their backs on these tumultuous years and make a new life in a very different world? Did they ever feel survivor guilt?

The early years in Canada were a time full of challenges for the young family. Life in a city like Winnipeg was strange for both CF and Mary. It stood in stark contrast to the villages of CF's youth, the cultured life of the cities where Mary grew up, and the life they had shared together in the city of Moscow. But the quiet daily life in the prairie city must have been a welcome respite from the turmoil of war and revolution in Russia. Did Mary miss the culture of her youth? And though she would have welcomed the chance to speak her native German in the wider family, did she miss the daily Russian conversation that had been familiar in the previous decade? But for now the task of raising her family was her main concern.

CF's family lived for the first couple of years in a house on Donald Street, shared by the Klassen siblings with their aging mother. The boy and girl that CF had jokingly talked about—mentioned in Mary's letter from Moscow—soon joined the family. On March 1, 1929, soon after their arrival in Canada, her third son, Herb was born. Two years later, on July 20, 1931, not one but two little girls were born!

Unfortunately, the health of the second twin, Tinalie, Irmy's sister, was a major concern for the next two years.

*CF and Mary with the Donald St. Klassen household in Winnipeg, 1929*

Tinalie was partially paralyzed from birth and never enjoyed a full and healthy life. But she had a sweet nature and was showered with affection by everyone, including her twin sister. Her health was deeply concerning to her parents, and often Mary carried that burden alone. The little frail girl died at the age of two and a half. The loss of her twin left deep wounds that probably affected Irmy in ways that were never fully understood. But life continued busily for Mary, with her family occupying an all-consuming focus.

In fact, during the 1930s and 1940s the family moved several times. In 1931, they moved to the western edge of Winnipeg called Woodhaven. Mary was grateful for the decision to move into a rental home where CF and Mary's family could be on their own. It was here that Harold started school. He spoke little English and was teased by the other children. This aroused Mary's protective instincts for her firstborn! But the teacher advised her to allow him to deal with the challenge in his own way; he gradually gained language skills and held his own.

*Klassen brothers in Winnipeg, 1929: back row, Alec, John, Jake, and Henry; front row, CF, Nick, and Franz*

The next move was to Seven Oaks on the north side of the city. It was there that Mary faced the crisis of Herb needing surgery for appendicitis at the age of two and a half. A further rental home in the North End at 476 Powers Street was remembered as the place where little Tinalie died. In this neighborhood the Klassens were surrounded by other immigrants, particularly an immigrant Jewish community. After renting another house at 119 Machray Avenue for an additional year, Mary became convinced that renting was not a good policy and insisted that it was time to purchase a home of their own.

She negotiated the purchase of a house at 165 Cathedral Avenue, which they bought from the Rev. Ernest Salter, a Methodist minister and director of the Bible Society in Winnipeg. Herb does not recall how the necessary funds were procured. The house was later sold and a house bought at 951 Henderson Highway in East Kildonan. This brought the number of Winnipeg houses that the Klassens called home to a total of six, before the move to British Columbia in 1948. Mary's large entrepreneurial capacity was clearly in evidence through all these moves!

*CF and Mary with Walfried, Harold, Herb, Irmy, and a friend in Winnipeg*

In all her challenges on the home front, with CF frequently traveling, Mary was always supported by family and wonderful friends like Ben and Esther Horch and Dr. Rudolph and Selma Claassen. In the KGB interrogation Jakob had mentioned Dr. Rudolph Claassen as part of their Moscow circle. He was a frequent presence in times of health needs in their home, especially with Tinalie. He also oversaw many routine medical matters like children's shots, which he came to administer at the Klassen home. He was also there to help in the emergency already mentioned: namely, my husband's appendix surgery. In the absence of a father, Herb says Dr. Rudolph felt like family.

When possible, CF was a doting father; he tried to organize family events and trips whenever he was at home. But he was also occupied with matters concerning his Mennonite people. In 1930, he had accompanied David Toews to the Mennonite World Conference in Danzig, Poland. Through his contacts with P.C. Hiebert, head of MCC, CF was sent on trips as a kind of ambassador to visit the Russian Mennonite immigrant communities in both the USA and Canada. It was a joy for him to see many that he had helped emigrate now peacefully settled in their new lives. He also visited Alvin Miller and his family in their home in Pennsylvania, renewing their friendship begun in Moscow. I'm sure the Millers were sorry that Mary could not share that trip and meet the family of the man for whom she had worked so hard in Moscow!

As consolation, CF, always an avid photographer, returned home with many photographs of the people and places he had visited. Any anxiety Mary had expressed to her mother-in-law about making a living in their new country was soon laid to rest when, in 1930, CF was recruited by David Toews for a three-month assignment. CF was to work as an assistant bookkeeper and cashier for the Canadian Mennonite Board of Colonization, which was administered by David Toews. The specific task was to collect the two-million-dollar *Reiseschuld* owed to the CPR. CF's short-term employment would eventually stretch to sixteen years. A celebration marking the final payment of that debt was held in 1946.

Over those years, the immigrant population, though decidedly not rich, took it as a matter of honor to repay every cent of the travel debt. For some, the small monthly payments were quite manageable. Many young women hired themselves to more wealthy Canadian families as housekeepers and nannies, in order to help their own families pay down the debt. But for some, particularly those who were having difficulty farming or simply earning a living, some resentment developed towards the man who constantly reminded them of their obligation. But they were faithful. The sacrifices of those years eventually proved worthwhile, a credit to both CF and Mary, and to the entire Mennonite community.

As CF called on the new immigrants, he reconnected with many that he had last seen passing through Moscow on their journey to a new homeland. He always had an excellent memory for names and details about different families—information that would prove invaluable in the next phase of service to his people.

One side-effect of CF's debt-collection assignment was that Mary was often left at home taking the responsibilities of parenthood alone, while he traveled across the country to the various Mennonite communities in Canada. When the children were small, she later told me, her entire life revolved around their needs. Often she was very weary and would go to bed herself as soon as her children were asleep. She rose early each day to take care of the running of the household and attending to the necessary tasks like stoking the furnace. Perhaps these years prepared her for the future years when CF would be gone for longer periods, months on end in Europe, and the eventual years alone as his widow.

In Winnipeg, however, Mary willingly helped with correspondence and accounting in the task of collecting the travel debt. Occasionally, she accompanied CF on shorter trips to outlying towns. She is remembered by some as always sitting outside in the car doing her *Handarbeit* (embroidery or knitting).

As accountant, she was responsible for the banking side of the debt collection. She recounts one memorable day in Winnipeg when she was on her way to the bank on the streetcar. At her stop she stepped out, but the sliding doors closed faster than she expected, trapping her bag of money and checks inside. When the streetcar moved off, she ran after it, gesticulating and trying to get the driver's attention. Thankfully, she reclaimed her bag of money when the streetcar stopped for her!

"C.F. Klassen could not have found a more valuable and competent wife in all the Mennonite villages in Russia," remarked J.B. Toews in a conversation that Herb and I had with him years later. JB, one of the eminent leaders among the Russian Mennonite people in Canada and the USA, knew CF and Mary very well. Not only had JB happened to be in Moscow to witness the marriage of CF and Mary many years earlier, but in the years that followed they also continued to be close friends. Mary worked hard on all fronts: community, church, and family. She was gradually earning acceptance among the people who had adopted her.

Mary continued to gain respect from the circle of friends in which she moved. She stood tall beside her husband, holding her head high in all phases of their life together. She even began to ask herself about the step of baptism into their community of faith in Winnipeg, the North End Mennonite Brethren Church. Their minister, C.N. Hiebert, had been a source of strength for Mary during the difficult time of Tinalie's sickness and death, when Mary had been reaching out for a stronger hold on her faith.

At that time, her youngest son, Herb, was attending the church kindergarten led by Esther Horch. He came home one day and sang to her this simple children's chorus:

*One door and only one,*
*And yet its sides are two;*
*I'm on the inside,*
*On which side are you?*

After all the years of upheaval and hard choices, Mary felt she was still an outsider to the faith community. But she knew she wanted to belong. Her heart was with the Mennonite community in all matters of the faith. So it seemed like a logical step to ask for the outward sign of baptism, to seal the inward step she had been taking for years, and to become fully part of the Mennonite people.

So, on August 4, 1935, in the presence of all, including her own young children, she took the step of baptism in the cold waters of the Assiniboine River to the great joy of her husband. Minister C.N. Hiebert officiated at the baptism and Minister Jakob Epp gave the message. That evening both CF and Mary were welcomed as members of the North End Mennonite Brethren Church, CF by transfer and Mary by baptism. CF's membership withdrawal from the Mennonite Brethren Church in Russia had been reinstated in 1929 when he arrived in Canada.

Mary had become a true Anabaptist as I would many years later. We shared the common bond of those baptized as babies, who are then re-baptized upon confession of faith.

As the storm clouds began to gather over Europe in the 1930s, the usual ties of Mennonites with all things German began to strain. Some of the more discerning Mennonites began to see a more ominous side to the rise of Hitler, in spite of the progress he was obviously fostering in the German homeland. Other Mennonites were slow to abandon their initial favorable opinions of the *Führer* and his hypnotic appeal. However, Mary sensed early on that a totalitarian state ruled by Hitler could not be good, choosing instead to express her sense of patriotism to her new country, Canada. She even had a record of *There'll always be an England* that she played on the phonograph at strategic moments, Canada being deeply loyal to England.

One of those moments happened in the Klassen home in connection with a letter that CF had written to the Royal Canadian Mounted Police (RCMP) in Winnipeg, making the case that the Mennonites were actually not German, but of Dutch descent. The RCMP were also aware that CF was counseling young men about how to assert their conscientious objector status, which could exempt them from military combat service. When an RCMP official came to the house to question him, Herb remembers his mother having that record on the phonograph as background music!

In 1936, those Dutch roots were the focus of a Mennonite World Conference in Amsterdam. At the invitation of Harold Bender, CF accompanied David Toews as Canada's representatives. In those days there was no question of Mary accompanying him on such a long and arduous trip, leaving her young family alone in Canada. So she had to await the glowing reports that he gave in the churches on his return. But CF made his mark on the Amsterdam conference with his concern for his abandoned brothers and sisters in Russia.

*CF, Mary, Harold, Walfried, Herb, and Irmy in Winnipeg, 1936*

Harold Bender's biographer, Albert N. Keim, relayed Bender's positive assessment of CF and his work among Mennonite refugees. According to Keim, "Klassen became a near-legendary figure in the Mennonite world . . . a paragon of integrity. By World War II, he was the best-known Mennonite in Canada. . . . A tall, broad-shouldered man who typically wore well-tailored double-breasted suits and a fedora hat, Klassen cut an impressive figure; he also exuded boundless energy, warm piety, and good common sense."[30]

I think Mary would have smiled wryly at such glowing descriptions of her husband and just shrugged them off with a comment like: *Ach, Cornelius!*

But I sometimes wonder how it felt for her to be married to such a distinguished figure in the Mennonite world and yet spend so little time with him as her husband and the father of their children? Did conflict ever arise over his commitment to the broader responsibilities to which he felt called?

*Herb, Irmy, and Harold, 1940s*

---

[30] Albert N. Keim, *Harold S. Bender (1897–1962)* (Scottdale: Herald Press, 1998), 472.

One thing is clear: Mary was strong enough to carry on her own shoulders the many responsibilities of family life. But scars from absentee fathering were probably there. And possibly there were some who criticized him for apparently neglecting his family. However, it is a tribute to Mary's strength and competence that family affairs like moving from one house to another, managing the children's education, and much more, were accomplished so well. At times she was forced to be both mother and father.

During the early years in Canada, I suspect there must have been times that Mary would have wondered about the ultimate fate of those whom she and CF had left behind in Russia. Did she ever wonder what had happened to Jakob? If she did, she never spoke about it. Still, fears about the state of affairs of those who had remained under Stalin's iron rule were beginning to trouble those who had reached the safety of life in Canada.

However, having heard nothing about Jakob in the long years of Mary's life in Canada as the wife of CF, she may well have had the sense that Jakob's difficult life was over. She could then be at peace, for only then could she face the many years ahead of her with her characteristic good humor and faith. She was a woman who put to rest the issues and burdens that might have been too heavy to bear. She had a life to live and many tasks to accomplish. She needed to summon all the courage she could muster, in order to face the challenges of what would be several more decades in her chosen country, Canada.

There were those close to Mary during the Winnipeg years who knew of her first marriage in Russia. As the children were growing up and going to school rumors surfaced. According to some of the cousins, Harold was sometimes teased by other children, who insinuated that he was not a real son of CF. This he hotly denied, since he had always felt proud to be a son of CF, and had always been treated as one. Finally, encouraged by CF's siblings, the couple decided to tell Harold the truth on his sixteenth birthday, as related earlier in this book.

## Post-War Years (1945–1954): CF to Europe

After World War II, it gradually became clear that many Mennonites had escaped with the fleeing German army and were now stranded in refugee camps in Europe. CF, as we have seen, was becoming well-known in the wider Mennonite family in North America. So in 1945, at the MCC meetings in Chicago, the call went out for someone to head up the work of contacting this group of people and helping them leave Europe. CF was a natural choice. One wonders how difficult the decision was for the busy family in Winnipeg to respond to that invitation.

In those years, there was no option for Mary to move her family to Germany and join him in that work, although CF's youngest sister, Elfrieda, and her husband, Peter Dyck, were later able to work side by side in refugee aid in Germany for many years.[31] Mary agreed that CF could take an exploratory trip to Europe, never realizing that the trip previewed to be several months would stretch to an assignment lasting almost nine years, with twenty-four Atlantic crossings over that span of time! She supported him from afar with many typed letters of news and reports about the children. I have sometimes wondered if "survivor guilt" played a part in CF's eagerness to return to Europe to help some of those who had been left behind when the door to emigration closed.

Mary never complained about her lonely life. She appreciated the help her husband was bringing to many more of his people. Her role was to continue the task of raising her family and caring for their many needs. Her spirit was strong and she never regretted their choice to make Canada home. As she had promised in Moscow, she saw to it that her two sisters, Irmgard and Erika, and their families, were able to immigrate to Canada.

Herb has no memory of there ever being difficult financial times during those years. But I have a hunch that behind the scenes, Mary found it challenging to raise her family with a husband far away and with funds not always available for all she needed. Her entrepreneurial gift occasionally took over as in the case of one of the many items they had somehow managed to bring with them to Canada from Russia—a carpet from the Tsar's palace. She sold it to T.O.F. Herzer, who was affiliated with the CPR and director of the Canada Colonization Association, a partner organization with the Canadian Mennonite Board of Colonization. CF worked with Herzer in the collection of the travel debt.

The reason why that sale is memorable in our family is that Mary often laughingly referred to that eminent gentleman—who incidentally shared her Lutheran background—as one whose name was an example of German pomposity. His initials, T.O.F., stood for Traugott Otto Frances, but Mary liked to say this was for *trau Gott, fürchte Gott*, which means, "trust God, fear God"! Quite a name to give to a baby!

---

[31] See Peter Dyck and Elfrieda Dyck, *Up From the Rubble: The Epic Rescue of Thousands of War-Ravaged Mennonite Refugees* (Scottdale: Herald Press, 1991).

## Life After Moscow

Mary was grateful to be surrounded in Winnipeg by many good friends and relatives who were already forming a wider community of social life and faith for herself and her growing family. Matters of education and cultural training began to take their full attention. Her children thrived in school and participated in various musical activities and church involvements. Harold, her firstborn, went on to enroll in the faculty of engineering at the University of Manitoba. I don't believe Mary ever told him that his father, Jakob, had chosen a same specialty, electrical engineering.

In addition to spending many months at a time alone with her children, Mary had to play hostess to the many visitors who besieged him at their home when he did return between trips. Playing hostess was not her favorite role in life as her culinary skills were not high on her list of priorities! Apparently, one of her favorite comments when such demands were placed on her was: "As long as we have bread and water, it is enough!" Tea could always be served. Yet she was always a gracious hostess, although she confessed later in life that she was often relieved when her husband had to leave again on his travels. Then she could be alone again, enabling her to revert to her quiet role as simply mother, something which gave her great satisfaction.

Whenever CF returned home from Europe, he was much in demand to give reports in the churches. This was the role that endeared him to so many as he brought news to them of loved ones from whom they had not heard for a long time. CF met them in German refugee camps, awaiting their journey to new homelands. In January 1950, he gave reports in Winnipeg, Saskatoon, Coaldale, and Abbotsford. CF's public life meant that Mary would have to graciously share her husband with others for long hours, just when she had so little time to help him catch up with family news and the lives of their children. But CF loved these opportunities to report on his work; his stories would keep church congregations in rapt attention for hours.

Some years ago, Herb and I wrote the following for an MCC presentation, describing this phase of CF's work in Germany. It was based on our research into CF's life and the recollections from local Abbotsford residents who immigrated during that time.

*It was a sunny Sunday morning in early autumn in Bavaria, West Germany. The year was 1945. A car was driving through a quiet village near the Czech border, stopping frequently as its driver and passenger looked around searching for something or someone. Suddenly strains of a hymn could be heard on the morning air:* Weiss ich den Weg auch nicht, Du weisst ihn Wohl [*Even when I don't know the way, You Lord, know it well*].

*Excitedly, the passenger, C.F. Klassen, explained, "Those are my people—let's go to them!"*

*Imagine the surprise and joy of the little group of Russian refugees crowded into a farm cottage with wide-open windows. They were comforting their hearts with familiar hymns from their lost homeland in Russia, when a tall stranger strode into the room—a Klassen from Canada—but speaking their native Low German dialect! He was one of them, who had also left Russia and gone to Canada in 1928. Now he had come to post-war Germany, "seeking his brothers and sisters," he said, offering them sponsorship from a Mennonite family in North America through MCC in order to find a new homeland.*

*His name became a harbinger of hope for thousands who passed through West Germany, with his characteristic word of encouragement, "Gott kann" [God can]. When all human efforts failed, he pointed people to a God who always cares for the homeless and orphans. And he always brought compassion and understanding to each one he met.*

Many of the Mennonites first leaving Europe after the war were sent to Paraguay. CF even spent a month in Paraguay to understand the conditions that would face emigrants he encouraged to settle there. Later more were cleared to come to Canada and USA. His work in Europe even extended to the hard task of caring for those who were not well enough to join their relatives in new homelands. These were housed in a series of new Homes for the Aged in Germany, which he continued to visit all his years in Germany. There was widespread support and interest in the churches of North America for this aspect of MCC's work, something that was fostered as CF toured the continent reporting and advocating for the Mennonite refugees right up to the year before his death.

How could Mary not rejoice that her husband could participate in such a work going forward? And surely she felt any sacrifices on the part of herself and her children were worthwhile in the long run. So, instead of lamenting the fact that she could not participate in that work herself, she occupied herself with other challenges that fit her entrepreneurial spirit. She began contemplating a move for the family that she had been left to manage in Winnipeg!

Once again Mary's take-charge capacity was called for. A word she often used when describing others was *unternehmungslustig*. It doesn't sound quite right in literal English, but translates as "enterprising." It truly fit her personality. In Moscow, Mary's farsightedness had prompted her persistent efforts to secure exit papers, enabling CF and Mary to finally leave Russia. Now in Winnipeg, there came a time when she had a strong sense that the family should move out to the west coast of Canada. CF's brothers Nick and Alec, and sister Justina, had already moved there. CF and Mary had made a few trips there as a family, and Mary was attracted to the milder climate and the lush growth she had seen in the beautiful Fraser Valley on her visits there. Perhaps the orchards and fragrant lilacs and acacias, as well as the stately evergreens, reminded her of her home in the Baltics, or the fragrance and beauty of Crimea.

At any rate, it was at her insistence that the decision to move to British Columbia was taken and it fell to her to plan and oversee the family move—no mean feat for a woman to manage on her own. Thus began the final chapter of her life, most of which was to be lived as a widow. She purchased a lovely home on elevated land overlooking the Fraser Valley in 1948, the year of a disastrous flood in the valley. This meant that they were able to offer refuge to some less fortunate residents from lower ground. But after a few tries at hobby farming with her young teenaged children, and a couple of other moves, she finally purchased the four-acre property on the edge of Clearbrook, where I first met her in 1959.

Mary told us she had been walking up the hill of Old Yale Road from the Mennonite high school, when she saw a "for sale" sign between the trees at the summit. Something told her that this was what she was looking for. The choice property poised between the town of Clearbrook below and the countryside beyond remained in the family for decades. Now it belongs to a non-profit society that houses the mission and retreat center called the *Mark Centre*, run by our son, Steve, and his wife, Evy.

Despite their many years of separation, CF did manage to share with Mary the joyful events of the weddings of his two oldest sons. Walfried married Helene Rempel on September 9, 1950, and on August 25, 1951, Harold married Ruth Thiessen, the daughter of one of CF's closest friends from Russia, F.C. Thiessen.

Then in September 1951, CF and Mary celebrated their twenty-fifth wedding anniversary at the gymnasium of the Mennonite high school in Abbotsford. It seems quite a feat for them to have managed to fit the event into his busy life! There were many speeches and well-wishes. The occasion was clearly used to express the gratitude of many for his thirty-five years of faithful service to his people. I wonder if that fact overshadowed the other milestone. But photographs of the day show them white-haired and joyful, standing together at last.

*Mary and CF on their twenty-fifth wedding anniversary, 1951*

With the move to British Columbia and the eventual purchase of the Old Yale Road property, the couple finally built a home that was to be the place of their retirement together, after all the busy years. But before this would be realized, a year together in Frankfurt was planned for 1953–1954. The couple took their two youngest children with them for what was to be CF's final year in Europe. The two college-aged children planned to study in Europe, while CF and Mary threw themselves into a busy life in Frankfurt, Germany.

Mary was glad to be able, at last, to join her husband in his important work. Many friendships and renewed acquaintances with people like Benjamin Unruh and Peter Froese were fostered during that year. After his release from Soviet custody in 1940, Froese had become a German language teacher in a school west of Moscow until the outbreak of World War II. On October 5, 1941, German forces took control of the town where he was teaching. From within the German occupation zone, Froese managed to secure travel documentation that took him out of Russia into Germany. He settled in Weinheim, near Heidelberg.

These reunions were especially precious for CF and Mary. She often joked that CF was too Europeanized to ever settle down happily in Canada. But she was hoping that at the end of this year in Germany, they would return as a family to Canada for a much earned rest and a happy retirement. Tragically, that was not to be.

One letter from this period recently came into our hands. It gives us Mary's voice, in the last year of her marriage to CF. It reveals some clear insights into her life at this juncture in the long saga of years of separation from her husband. She is writing to her brother and sister-in-law, Franz and Katja Klassen, who had just moved from Winnipeg to British Columbia. It is dated January 14, 1954, just five months before CF's death.[32]

*CF and Mary in Frankfurt, Germany, 1954*

The style, similar to her Moscow letters, is chatty and rambling. She wrote as she thought, busy at her typewriter in Frankfurt,

---

[32] A copy of Mary's letter, dated January 14, 1954, is included in the the Mary Brieger Klassen personal papers collection, Centre for Mennonite Brethren Studies, Winnipeg.

composing letters and helping CF in his work. Here we see Mary the congenial sister-in-law, Mary the optimist, Mary the forgiver, Mary the philosopher, poetry-lover, and woman of faith!

*Dear Franz and Katja, your letter from December 14th gave us great joy! There's nothing nicer for us here than to receive letters from you all, our dear family in Canada! What wonderful bonds we enjoy through the postal service. How terrible if the ocean could so separate us that we could not hear from one another. I can't imagine it. How happy we are when we hear news of our dear children and grandchildren. Thank God you are all safe and well, something we can't take for granted, when we are all so far apart, spread out around the world.*

*And if once in a while we suffer a bit of ill health, it gives God a chance to graciously help us again.*

*We are thankful that Cornelius is well again and that he can do his work again. He took to his bed for a while, but will soon be active again. I have to type a letter for him. I am so happy I can help him a little, which makes me think how terrible it is that he has worked here for eight years without the help of his family. But who would have thought it? He went off for one trip and the work has lasted eight years! But I am praying that we can spend the last years together in Canada, not in Europe.*

She then goes on to describe how pleasant life is in Europe and how grateful both the Germans and the Americans are for the work her husband is doing.

She continues to describe her own state of mind.

*Yes it's all very good, but for me, I long for home, and I continue to pray that Cornelius could finish his work here and return to Canada to work . . .*

*So wonderful that you have become BCers! Too bad your children are still in Manitoba. Why do things have to be that way? But we have to leave it all in God's hands. He orders everything for the best. I am still amazed that I am here in Germany. I did nothing to arrange it. He has ordered it all.*

Speaking of CF's life in Germany, she writes:

*Cornelius has many friends here. It makes me a little anxious that he will feel so close to his friends here and that he will forget all the good friends he has in Canada. Hopefully not, since so many write to us here, and I enjoy receiving the letters so much!*

She continues describing the weather in Germany and the scenery which she finds very pleasant. "Not much rain, it had just *gedrizeldt* a little"—her word! She admires the orderly land, the majestic trees, the vineyards and forests, the spacious squares and beautiful houses. But she still sees the scars of war.

*There are many destroyed houses. How heartbreaking! It is terrible to think that people just like us lived there. It makes me weep to think of it. Poor people and so many of them had no trust in God, no eternal hope! Ah, that is so sad! How thankful we should be that we have a God whom we trust and a Savior who cares for us! Do we really intercede for our fellow human beings? Do we care from the heart, not just lip service? May God be merciful to us all and help us. We can do nothing without Him!*

*CF, Irmy, Mary, and Herb in Frankfurt, Germany, 1954*

    She continues with more details about their life in Frankfurt, and their attendance at the beautifully restored Lutheran Church, where CF really appreciates Pastor Gottwaldt. They wish that they could record his sermons and bring them home for the rest of the family to enjoy! She writes about Irmy's musical studies, including her singing of the liturgy at church. She writes about Herb's studies in Basel and her gratitude that he has chosen that place to study (under Karl Barth!) rather than Heidelberg. In Basel there is a strong Mennonite presence, including the MCC home that enables him to participate in many activities. Committing her two youngest children to the Lord, she says:

*Hopefully, in this short time, they will both study hard and learn a lot with no negative influences coming into their lives. Not that we can protect our children, nor is it so different in Canada, but for myself, I do feel the best thing would be to go back home to Canada as soon as we can. Oh, I'm such a homebody and will probably be that way until the end of my life! What do I need at my age with a lot of traveling around and seeing places! It's all the same to me, and our Heavenly Father has created every part of this earth, whether we call it Canada or Italy or Spain. Their existence all seems like a fairy tale to me! "Die Welt ist vollkommen all überall, wo der Mensch nicht hinkommt mit seiner Qual" [The world is perfectly ordered everywhere, except where people leave their evil mark].*

The letter concludes with some family politics. Mary was always known for her warmth and love towards every member of the extended family. Her in-laws were just enjoying welcoming a new daughter-in-law into the family for their son Frank. A slight oversight had meant that CF and Mary did not receive the invitation in Frankfurt, something that Mary dismisses lightly and graciously, avoiding any potential slight.

*And Frankie is married, and you have a beloved new daughter-in-law. I really love her, and her whole family, the Aaron Rempels. And of course we have one of Abram Rempel's daughters for our daughter-in-law, our Helene (Walfried's wife). And your Ruth has always impressed me as a very motherly person, being the eldest in the family. So, I'm happy for you, now that she is your daughter. I believe she will respect you. I am so glad we were in Winnipeg this past winter and were able to get to know these young people. And your girls also have good husbands. What a blessing! It's hard to say which one is the best; they are both such fine young men! God is so good to us and we have so much to thank Him for. Please do give them all our love next time you write to them.*

*And naturally it doesn't matter at all that you didn't send us an invitation to Frankie and Ruth's wedding. We totally understand; and anyway we couldn't have come! We've been through a lot worse than that in our lives, so we should never make big elephants out of such little matters! We realize that in our scattered existence, we are all frequently out of touch with each other; and everyone is forgetful of something sometime or another.*

*I'm glad you like your VW. Everyone here loves them! I can't wait to go for a ride with you in yours! My heart leaps every time I think about returning to Canada. I must get everything here organized first, and finish everything. There's nothing like Canada, nothing like the CPR. I would be so happy if CF could work for them again!*

*We think of you always with love and look forward to a reunion of our families very soon and to good health for all! Without Him we are nothing.*

*Greetings to Nick and Irma, Justina and Mietja, and all their families. My heart always warms at the thought of each one of you!*

## Life After Moscow

*With heartfelt love, we greet all of you, your Cornelius and Mary.*

Sadly, all the good wishes for a healthy return to Canada as a family were not to be. On May 8, 1954, CF had a heart attack in Gronau en route to a Peace Conference in Holland. Gronau, on the border between Germany and Holland, was a refugee camp where all the work of processing Mennonites seeking emigration had begun.

On hearing the news, Mary rushed there from Frankfurt, but arrived too late. He had died in the night, calling out her name. He was fifty-nine.

His death left many reeling in shock, and left a huge gap in the refugee relief work of MCC in Europe. The funeral, at the Nord Ost Lutheran Church in Frankfurt, was an impressive occasion with many from France, Switzerland, Holland, Germany, and North America remembering CF's life and ministry. After the funeral, Mary returned home to her retirement in Canada, a widow. She was accompanied by her daughter, Irmy, but her son, Herb, followed two months later after completing his studies in Basel.

## Mary Alone Again

Once more, circumstances required Mary to make another life adjustment during the remaining years of her sojourn on this earth, and she did so with her usual characteristic energy and good faith. Never one to pity herself, she shunned the very idea of joining a *Witwen Verein* (widows' circle), though she did provide warmth and hospitality to many who found themselves in that life circumstance.

In June 1956, Mary's daughter, Irmy, was married. She had met Vance George during her time studying at Goshen College in Indiana. This time Mary was in charge of the event alone. Adding to the stress, this was just after Harold had been diagnosed with a life-threatening brain tumor. Mary did the best she could. I recently discovered that a carpet she had made and sold to her friend in Yarrow was sold for $25 in order to help pay for the wedding. The wedding was held at the South Abbotsford Mennonite Brethren Church. Soon after the wedding, the couple left to teach in India for three years at Woodstock School. Mary had no daughter close by for many years.

However, again in her enterprising style, she used her home to provide a home for a group of students studying at the nearby Mennonite high school. Her "girls," as she called them, remember their time under her roof and under her wing with warmth and humor; they were grateful for her loyalty to them in all circumstances!

One of them recalls a time when Mary had a box of chocolates placed on the piano in her living room. The girls occasionally took these delicious morsels without asking. Later during a spiritual renewal week at their school, they repented and humbly confessed their actions to Mary, who most graciously forgave them and laughingly restored them to the warmth of her motherly care!

The time came when Mary decided to divide her acreage in half to provide room for Harold to build a home for his young family. Walfried lived close by with his rapidly growing family. Mary was glad to have them near. Eventually, she sold her large home and had Herb build her a more modest one behind Harold's where she could live on her own. This was the "glasshouse" where I first met her; it was her would-be dacha. This is where she would spend the remaining years of her life.

My husband was at that time working in the architectural department at the University of British Columbia library, filing journals about the new West Coast designs in architecture. He adapted some of these designs for his mother's new home, with two walls of glass and huge cedar beams. Some of her friends were surprised at the different kind of home she was planning to live in, but she liked the daring architectural style.

This home would be the context where she would entertain her many guests in her final years. It was also the home she shared with us during our early years in Canada described at the beginning of this book, with the addition of the little cabin at the back. It was here that she gathered around herself the remaining mementos of her journey, and reflected on the many experiences of her varied life. And it was here I would begin to pick up some of the clues about her life, clues to what was never verbalized in our time together.

In her collection of china, Mary had several plates with the Russian royal insignia, which we were told came from the Tsar's palace. She rarely used them and we never discussed how they were procured, nor how she had managed to bring them intact to Canada! We still have the plates in our extended family!

I can still picture Mary from those years in her lovely home on the hill, overlooking her lilac hedge; she is sitting on her deck, pouring tea for her children and grandchildren and her many guests. She would be serving us her signature apple cake that included apples she had gleaned from local friends on her walks through Clearbrook.

These were busy years as she worked for Dr. Buirs as his receptionist. But they were also hard years as she tried to help her daughter through a difficult marriage crisis and subsequent divorce. She deeply regretted the severe health conditions that followed Irmy's divorce and spent many hours praying for her daughter. One image I recall is of Mary walking the long driveway of her property, wringing her hands in prayer and speaking the name of her daughter, Irmy, over and over.

The time came when Irmy's condition led to her hospitalization in a private psychiatric clinic in New York. With Mary's encouragement, the family decided that Herb should fly there and drive his sister home in a rental car with all her possessions. Irmy lived a challenging life back in British Columbia, working at times as a librarian in Prince Rupert and Delta, until her untimely death on August 8, 1979.

Mary always grieved the broken marriage of her daughter. But there was a deep bond between them forged through their shared suffering. And during the years after Mary's stroke in 1971, it was Irmy who went daily to the Menno Hospital and read to her mother, helping in her care.

I recall a remark Mary made to me once when someone had spoken negatively about her daughter's husband, "People shouldn't talk that way about him. He was her husband and they loved one another." Many years later I recalled that remark as I reflected on Mary's own life and memory of Jakob. I believe such goodwill extended to him, too.

Jakob's life was a chapter that it seemed would be forever closed in the circles of the Klassen family. His brief life was by now a distant memory, except for the destiny he shared with countless other Russian Mennonites who had made the critical choice, or who had been forced to accept the consequences of remaining in Russia.

After suffering her stroke, Mary spent her remaining years in the Menno Hospital in Abbotsford, requiring skilled nursing care. This fine facility, part of the Menno Place network, is similar to the many Homes for the Aged that CF helped to start in Germany. Mary died at the Menno Hospital on December 6, 1976, at the age of eighty-five.

## The Cameo

As I reflect on the life Mary lived in her Clearbrook house, I recall the ambience of the home with its works of art and embroidery, its tapestries and music. I think of the gramophone records playing the beautiful song cycle by Schumann, *Dichterliebe* (A Poet's Love) and wonder if they reminded her of the days long ago in Riga—*Im wunderschönen Monat Mai* (In the Beautiful Month of May), when love was birthed in the heart of a young girl. And when she played her Russian folk songs on her piano, including the Lermontov one about a lonely figure on the highway, what was she thinking about? I am glad I have the CD with Anna German singing that song, and a modern version of *Dichterliebe* sung by Dietrich Fischer-Dieskau. Mary's old 78s are long gone; but I still treasure her collection of Russian music, carefully preserved in a thick wallpaper cover that now sits near our piano.

During her lifetime, Mary was always giving items of her possessions away. She especially did this when any of her children expressed a particular interest in something. Other artifacts, like some beautifully sculpted black horses, have been handed down in the family as has CF's stamp collection and his rare coin collection, including some valuable Russian gold coins. But Mary had not apportioned her remaining jewelry items before her death.

Several of these were sentimentally valuable to us, because of their personal connection. In particular, she had a number of lovely Russian cameos. One was a beautifully crafted pendant. Mary is seen wearing it in many of the later photographs in Canada. It was only by a strange fluke that any of these mementos ever survived for us at all.

When Mary died, her jewelry remained for a time in the possession of her daughter, Irmy. After Irmy's death, it seemed at first that the jewelry was nowhere to be found. As we were sorting through our sister's belongings, suddenly a great shriek arose from Ruthie, Harold's wife, who was cleaning out the freezer. For there, carefully wrapped and sealed in a box, were some of the family heirlooms, including the two cameos, together with various rings and necklaces. Apparently, Mary and Irmy had thought the freezer was the last place a thief would go hunting for valuables! And indeed, it had been the last place we would have expected to find such mementos of Mary's life—another example of her ingenuity!

We all felt special care and respect were due these objects, and each piece was duly assigned. Because Herb and I were at that time engaged in a halfway house ministry, we felt such valuables should not reside with us, so Ruthie became the custodian of the cameo pendant, offering that I could borrow it any time I wished. Walfried's wife, Helene, received one of the cameo brooches.

*Mary's cameo*

The cameo pendant, however, has another story of its protected life before it came into my care. It was a little adventure that happened several years later. Ruthie had lent it to her daughter for a special occasion, but had forgotten that she had done so. One day Ruthie's house was broken into and some trinkets were stolen from the box where the cameo was usually kept. Ruthie was very upset, thinking that the cameo had been stolen. A few days later her daughter telephoned to say that she had returned the cameo while her mother was away, placing it in Ruthie's underwear drawer for safekeeping! Once again the cameo was kept safe.

In 2001, after our Russia years, when Ruthie lay dying, Herb and I went to pay her a final visit. The family was gathered around her bed.

There were tears, but also much gratitude for the hand of God's grace in all our lives. She was at peace, having accomplished many of the final tasks that she had set for herself in these final months, including a photo story of Harold's life for his children, with pictures of his reunion with his long-lost sister Erika. But Ruthie felt one small act remained to be done. She wanted to give the cameo into my keeping, until I could pass it on to the next custodian. She gave it to me with tears as we embraced for the last time.

The cameo for me is a token of the life that was left behind in Russia, a symbol of the elegant culture and beautiful life that became an all too distant memory. I wear it today whenever I want to evoke memories of all that was, and in honor of Mary's memory.

I received the cameo gratefully from Harold's widow, remembering those brief but momentous weeks when Harold and Ruthie came to Moscow to visit Erika for the first time. For me it was also a token of the task that I felt was entrusted to me, to trace more of the details of the life of the one who had worn the cameo, our beloved mother, Mary Brieger Klassen.

It was not given to Mary to participate directly in the earth-shattering events that took CF's attention for most of his years. But like Dorothea in George Eliot's *Middlemarch*, Mary's influence was a different kind: "her full nature spent itself in deeds which left no great name on the earth, but the effect of her being on those around her was incalculable."

My memories of my mother-in-law are overwhelmingly happy ones. I recall her happy chatter, her laughter and stories, her antics with her grandchildren, and her jokes about herself and the rest of us. I also recall her heartfelt prayers for us all, her generous forgiving spirit, and her resolute faith that all life's events would somehow be woven together for good in the Divine Economy.

However, there were also silences in Mary's life—untold stories and long-kept secrets. As I have reflected on her last long silence, since the stroke she experienced in 1971, the following scene came to me as a closing benediction on her life.

## Menno Hospital, 1976

Mary Brieger Klassen, now in her eighties, is resting in her bed, awaiting the arrival of her supper and of her daughter, Irmy, who will help the nursing staff by assisting in the feeding of her bedridden mother.

## Life After Moscow

The frail-looking woman is propped up on the pillow, with her eyes closed. The warm summer evening brings the light fragrance of the lilacs outside on the driveway through her open window. The clatter of food trolleys has not yet begun. Most visitors have left, so there is a pleasant lull in the day's activity. The old woman is in a state of reverie, a state which consumes most of her life these days.

Images from her past float in and out of her consciousness like gentle birds. Fragments of songs suggest themselves to her mind, but leave before her memory can capture more than the odd phrase. Poems from her childhood jostle with words of hymns from her youth. Smells of flowers like this lilac remind her of scenes from the far distant Crimea, which swiftly give way to images of cities not seen for over half a century—St. Petersburg, Riga, Moscow.

However, no songs issue from her mouth, and no poems will be spoken by this woman once known for her amazing memory. All has been silenced by the stroke that occurred a few years previously. Silenced also are the unspoken memories, the unshared stories, and the long-protected secrets of this woman's life.

As she awaits her daughter, do her thoughts reflect the sadness that has overtaken this gifted, intelligent woman, whose life is now slowly ebbing away? But even in this helpless state, this woman, a mere shadow of her former vibrant, energetic self, will not allow sad thoughts to dominate. Gratitude begins to flow over her like a wave from the deep Baltic Ocean where her life began. She allows it to immerse her being, as she quietly welcomes it to flow into the crevices of memory and images. The waves of gratitude begin to touch the remembrances that present themselves unbidden—the struggles and pain of her youth, the failed marriage with her first husband, the difficult loss of a child, her daughter's divorce, and the long separations from her second husband during his years of work in Europe.

A tear begins to fall across her cheek, but her motionless hands cannot wipe it away. Who will interpret such a tear, when no words can accompany it, or answer the inevitable questions? "Mary, are you tired of waiting for your tea? Do you wish your daughter would hurry up and come? Are you in pain, or uncomfortable?"

Perhaps more perceptive questioners might ask, "Mary, is something troubling you? Are you sad about something? Does something grieve your spirit? Do you harbor some deep regrets?"

The tear trickles down the parchment-like cheek. There will be no answers. There will never be any more answers in this life. But the spirit of this weary warrior, this courageous, witty and warm-hearted woman, shouts to us across the years with words that come to us in other ways than by human speech.

*I have lived my life as best I could.*
*It has been a very good life.*

*My tears are tears of joy and gratitude.*
*I could not have asked for more.*

*I have been blessed far beyond anything that I could have ever asked.*

*Where I have been hurt by others, I have forgiven them all long ago.*
*And where I have caused anyone pain, I trust I have been forgiven.*

*I have known much joy and happiness.*
*I am blessed with wonderful friends and family.*
*I have been given material and spiritual abundance.*

*I await my meeting with my Maker in peace,*
*And whatever reunions with those who have gone before that He might grant me.*

*May peace be upon us all.*

*Amen.*

# Epilogue: Messiah in the Kremlin

As I have reflected on the many fragments portrayed in the pages of this memoir, one very meaningful memory of our years in Moscow has repeatedly come to me. It is a strongly reconciling image. It occurred on an extraordinary occasion—the first performance of Handel's *Messiah* in Moscow after the dissolution of the Soviet Union. Herb and I were privileged to attend the event in, of all places, the Kremlin, the onetime stronghold of atheistic Soviet communism!

Growing up in England, I was familiar with Handel's *Messiah*, since my family always attended a performance of it during the Christmas season. As a believer, the strong prophetic words combined with Handel's beautiful music always affected me deeply.

Coming to Canada, I learned that Mennonites also loved these great German choral masterpieces. Harold's wife, Ruthie, was the daughter of F.C. Thiessen, a well-known choir director who led choirs both in Russia and Canada. And Harold and Ruthie's son, Randy, Jakob Reimer's grandson, would later direct college and church choirs in performances of Handel's *Messiah*. So, in a strange way, attending this particular performance drew together the diverse strands of this memoir.

In a deeper way, however, my memory of the event itself on that chilly November night in 1992 stands as a fitting conclusion to the many unanswered questions presented by the lives of those in the foregoing pages.

It was a cold snowy night when we walked across Red Square and went through the Kremlin gates, entering the Palace of Congresses, right inside that ancient Kremlin fortress. Little did I realize what a contemporary ring the time-honored prophetic words of *Messiah* would hold for the eager crowd that had gathered that evening. I had heard those words countless times before in England and Canada. But the full impact they held for the people of Russia, finally emerging from seventy years of communist domination, was unmistakable. Nor have I ever witnessed an audience response so fresh, so full of hope and expectation.

At center stage stood a massive menorah as if to symbolize God's promise of deliverance for an oppressed people. The conductor that evening was, of all people, Yehudi Menuhin, an ironic choice in the land that had silenced most of its gifted Jews for decades. He would not live much longer after this event. The choir was clad in somber robes reflecting the generations of suffering.

A dark-robed figure stepped forward and sang the prophetic words: "I will shake the heavens and the earth . . . all nations I will shake." That very shaking had begun in the 1980s as nation after nation in Eastern Europe had witnessed the crumbling of communism. And now Russia was being shaken. Had they longed for Him whom they were forbidden to worship? "Behold, darkness shall cover the earth, and deep darkness the people."

It seemed a graphic depiction of those dark years under Stalin. How deeply that darkness had penetrated the souls of this nation, living literally in "the land of the shadow of death."

Then came the words of the promise, "The people that walked in darkness have seen a great light." What impact could those words have on those who had lived so long under that darkness?

As I listened that night to the familiar chorus, "For unto us a child is born, unto us a Son is given," I was suddenly aware that the promise was coming, possibly for the first time, to a new "us," to a population that had never owned those promises. I had heard those words many times, but now "unto us" meant Russia, too! A Son was being given to many who had never called upon His name here, as only a minority had retained a memory of *Messiah's* promise through the Soviet era. What might it mean now for His name to be called "Wonderful, Counselor, the Everlasting Father, the Prince of Peace"?

Russia had known the fatherhood of tsars and dictators. Lenin's bones were still entombed outside the very walls of the Kremlin where we sat that cold night. But the Messiah arose from His tomb and still lives! He is a Leader, and a Father, totally unlike all the leaders of communism, one who will "feed His flock like a shepherd, and gently lead those with young." What a different image of leadership this presented than the clenched fist and the firing squad.

Then, coming to the heart of the oratorio that night, the words of the next chorus struck a new chord with me, "Behold, the Lamb of God that taketh away the sins of the world."

## Epilogue: Messiah in the Kremlin

We were sitting there in the shadow of seventy years of humanity's inhumanity—years of disappeared fathers, forced labor camps, exile, mass graves, systemic disinformation, starvation and purges, deprivations and death, a regime of endless lies and deception. Could the Lamb truly take away all that?

The reassurance came in the words, "Surely, He hath borne our griefs and carried our sorrows, the chastisement of our peace was upon Him and with His stripes we are healed." Reaching the climax of the performance, the Hallelujah chorus also had a new ring that night. The audience, unfamiliar with our Western traditions of standing to honor this moment, stayed respectfully in their seats, not knowing what to expect. They remained spellbound by this overwhelming song of praise to Jehovah, the King of Kings and Lord of Lords, who will reign forever and ever—longer than Stalin, or Krushchev, or Gorbachev. But at the close of the triumphant chorus, they leapt to their feet in spontaneous and genuine applause and excitement.

I recall that as we made our way back to our apartment from that momentous evening through the snow-filled streets of Moscow, I had a deep sense that things were going to be different in this beloved land of Russia from now on. I was grateful that we had glimpsed the beginning of that change.

I reflected that as we seek for a resolution to all the loose ends of our lives and our stories, to their broken pieces and torn fragments, we can acknowledge that the resolution does not lie with us. It rests in the hands of the One who continues to come afresh, as He did that cold night in Moscow.

# Acknowledgments

I am truly grateful to the many people who have had a part in bringing this book to completion. It has been almost two decades since that first telephone call in Moscow set this story in motion. Several people in particular have helped Herb and me along the way as we waited for all the pieces to come together, the pieces that make up this memoir of discovery.

My thank you list begins with Art DeFehr, who approached MCC in the late 1980s with a proposal to partner with a new business venture called Soviet Union Network. MCC agreed to the partnership and sent us to Russia to facilitate it. We are grateful to MB Mission for helping us return to Moscow after my accident in 1994 to complete our fifth year.

Then there are the two women without whom there would be no story: Mary Brieger Klassen, my mother-in-law, and Erika Reimer Gurieva, our newfound sister. They are the heart of this story. Knowing them has brought depth and meaning to the experience of Russia shared in these pages.

I am also immeasurably indebted to those in Russia who shared their lives and struggles with us during those difficult years of transition, 1990–1995. The Russian people and their culture have truly enlarged our hearts during these later years of our lives. They provided the impetus to write this story, which is the story of our family, too.

Herb and I were happy to respond to Harvey Dyck's invitation to return to Russia and help launch the Mennonite Centre of Ukraine in 2001. During this time we were able to reconnect with Erika and fill in more pieces of the story. Harvey's wife, Anne Konrad Dyck, inspired us all with her untiring pursuit of the stories of her relatives who remained in Russia.

Many in my wider family and beyond have encouraged me over the years to record what happened to us in Moscow. I thank them for their support. They have patiently listened to a "non-ethnic"

Mennonite try her hand at telling the Russian Mennonite story. Even if they know it very well, they were still willing to hear my perspective.

I am especially grateful to my nephew, Randy, Harold's son, for his support in writing the delicate story of his father and his grandfather, Jakob Reimer, Mary Brieger's first husband. I value Randy's help in getting some of the facts of the story clear, and his support in recording what we learned about his grandfather's life and tragic death. Randy's sincere appreciation of the project has made us feel that recording the story has been worthwhile.

There were also many others who gave me help and counsel early on in the process.

Rudy Wiebe was one of the first to encourage me to tell the facts, instead of trying to fictionalize the story. I can still hear him, "You have a fascinating story. Just tell it like it is. Fact is stranger than fiction."

My friend and fellow writer on Pender Island, Dorothy Siebert, helped me shape the story in the early stages, encouraging me to share some of my own journey, too. She helped me find my voice and make it more understandable in acceptable Canadian style, without too many archaic British-isms, like hitherto and henceforward!

John B. Toews read an earlier draft and loaned me a translation of the AMLV minutes. Conversation with John helped me get a better grasp of CF and Mary's struggle during that crucial post-Revolution period for the Mennonites in Russia.

Connie Braun, my former student at MEI, now an accomplished writer herself, read an early version of the manuscript also and gave me lots helpful advice. I am grateful for her encouragement to persevere and bring the book to completion.

My nephew, Neil, did the painstaking work of scanning the old album photographs to bring them to us in freshness and clarity. Most of the photographs in the book, and those used on the cover, are his careful work. My son, Mark, and his brother-in-law, Paul Janzen, helped me with the photographs on pages 20, 22, 25, 53, 55, 81, 112, 134, and 167. The photograph on page 72 is courtesy of the Centre for MB Studies, Winnipeg, and the photograph on page 73 comes from the Mennonite Heritage Centre, Winnipeg.

Herb and I are grateful to Mrs. Lilya Willms, a local Russian speaker, who helped us clarify our translation of Erika's letter that reproduced the interrogation transcript of Jakob's trial.

I give special thanks to the Mennonite Brethren Historical Commission and my initial contact, Andrew Dyck, for their early interest in a story "by and about MB women." I am grateful to them for considering the book for publication and for their decision to underwrite the whole venture.

I very much appreciated conferring with the two women on the Commission, Dora Dueck and Valerie Rempel. They offered much valued coaching on the art of story-telling and on the genre of memoir. Dora also helped me greatly in the final stages of editing.

My greatest thanks are to Jon Isaak, the Executive Secretary of the Commission, who took on the daunting role of being my editor, and did it with such grace and goodwill. It was a pleasure to share in the project together. I am indebted to him for his long patience with me. I greatly valued his attention to detail and history. He helped me to be faithful to my own perspective, while still leaving the final assessment to the reader.

My deepest thanks are to my ever-faithful family, Steve and Evy, Becky and Greg, Matt and Cathlyn, who have lived patiently with their mother's project through this whole phase of our life back in Canada. The two more directly involved were Tanya, my book-loving daughter, and Mark, my writer son (www.namesake.ca). Mark gave me advice, practical suggestions, and technical help, which seemed to be frequently needed.

And then there is my husband, Herb, who shared those wonderful and sometimes challenging years in Moscow with me. I am grateful for his constant support as we have lived with this story and for his unfailing patience and love at all times.

In addition to the Mennonite writers recognized in the footnotes, I am deeply indebted to the many Russian writers—Leo Tolstoy, Boris Pasternak, Yelena Bonner, Anna Akhmatova, and others—who greatly expanded my understanding of life in Russia during the 20th century.

There are no doubt still mistakes and inaccuracies that remain in the text, in spite of my best efforts to wrestle down the chronologies and details of this complex story. I thank all those who helped in the final editing stage, alerting me to problem areas and making helpful suggestions. I especially thank Anne Konrad and Peter Letkemann for their sharp eyes that saved me from some historical inaccuracies. For the errors that remain, I apologize, taking full responsibility for the text.

And the final word of thanks belongs to God, who allowed me to live long enough to bring this task to completion. His grace is amazing!

Maureen S. Klassen<br>April 2013